A GOD
FOR
SCIENCE?

Translator's Note

I am deeply indebted to the Very Reverend Fr. Hirlary, O.F.M.Cap., for reading this translation and suggesting many improvements. I also owe a debt of gratitude to Mrs. Ruth McIntyre for typing the manuscript.

PAUL BARRETT, O.F.M.CAP.
La Canada, California.

A God for Science?

by
JEAN-MARIE AUBERT

Translated by
Paul Barrett, O.F.M.Cap.

BL
240.2
A88

ST. JOSEPH'S UNIVERSITY   STX
BL240.2.A88   A God for science?

3 9353 00003 2878

106147

NEWMAN PRESS

Westminster, Md.   New York, N. Y.   Glen Rock, N. J.

Amsterdam   Toronto

A God for Science? is a translation of the French *Recherche Scienti-fique et Foi Chrétienne* by Jean-Marie Aubert, first published by Librairie Arthème Fayard, Paris. Copyright © Librairie Arthème Fayard, Paris, 1964.

NIHIL OBSTAT:
Fr. Hilarius a Graigcullen, O.F.M.Cap.
Censor theol. deput.

IMPRIMI POTEST:
Fr. Conradus a Leap, O.F.M.Cap.
Min. Prov. Hib.

June 26, 1966

NIHIL OBSTAT:
Very Rev. Msgr. Carroll E. Satterfield, J.C.D.
Censor Librorum

IMPRIMATUR:
✠ Lawrence Cardinal Shehan
Archbishop of Baltimore

May 22, 1967

The Nihil Obstat and Imprimatur are official declarations that a book or pamphlet is free of doctrinal or moral error. No implication is contained therein that those who have granted the Nihil Obstat and Imprimatur agree with the contents, opinions or statements expressed.

Copyright © 1967 by
The Missionary Society
of St. Paul the Apostle
in the State of New York

Library of Congress
Catalogue Card Number: 67-23605

Published by Newman Press
Editorial Office: 304 W. 58th St., N.Y., N.Y. 10019
Business Office: Westminster, Maryland 21157

Printed and bound in the
United States of America

CONTENTS

INTRODUCTION

A Matter of Conscience

The idea of writing this book came to me after reading a letter from a young engineer friend of mine who described in detail the problem he was having in reconciling his role as a scientist with his life as a Catholic. Because his difficulty had become a real matter of conscience for him, perhaps it would be better to let him speak for himself: "You have heard of the trouble we've been having in regulating the pile. [My friend is engaged in building an experimental nuclear pile for a government agency]. I have tackled the problem energetically and enthusiastically because I know what it represents—making a contribution to greater control of nuclear energy, which is so important for the future, and having the satisfaction of penetrating more deeply into the mystery of matter. Only now am I coming to realize just how exhilarating my work is, and I feel that I'm committed to it body and soul. . . .

"But unfortunately for me, it is just at this very point that I have begun to get qualms of conscience, about which I want to talk to you right away. While I was a student, and even when I began to practice as a young engineer without any great responsibilities, I had very little difficulty in reconciling my faith and my scientific work. But since then there have been many changes, and my present life has become so full that I feel no need for anything apart from my work and my love for Christine [his young wife]. I am speaking very simply and without any false shame when I say that I have the impression that my religious life has been reduced to a minimum of loose ties to God, and that I continue practicing

1

my faith simply out of fidelity to the religion that I have always professed and so as not to displease my wife. . . .

"I must tell you that I have become aware of this new state of affairs only recently, and it was a great shock to me. Here is how it happened. A few Sundays ago I was attending Mass in a neighboring village. I had gone to bed late the night before, because I had been finishing up a report on a suggestion I had made about a modification to cut down on the number of access ports in the nuclear pile by passing both the uranium rods and the control rods through the same ports. So I must admit that I was attending Mass in body only, for my mind was so absorbed in my suggestion and its advantages that I was not in the least following what was going on at the altar. I couldn't even have told you what the sermon was about.

"I was suddenly awakened from my daydreaming by my wife, who interrupted my reverie when she got up to go to communion. It was then that I literally woke up and became conscious of where I was and what was happening. At the same instant, I had the feeling that all of it was terribly far away, that I had become a stranger to the world of religion that surrounded me. The gestures of the priest then seemed so devoid of meaning that I was a little frightened. I thought of Claudel's conversion, but in reverse, as it were: he, a literary man, a poet, who did not believe, had suddenly received the light of faith after listening to ecclesiastical chant; while I, on the contrary, a believing scientist—as I imagined myself—had received a completely contrary "illumination" in a church. I need not tell you that I take no pride in the comparison, but am instead greatly humiliated and troubled by it.

"When I came out of the church, and during the days that followed, I thought almost constantly about what I had just experienced. I recalled the remarks of an engineering colleague of mine —an atheist and more or less a Marxist—with whom I became acquainted last year. He said that religion is probably a stage of development that we had outgrown; that it once was useful, no doubt, but that it is no longer able to meet the demands of the modern world. 'It's a mere matter of sentiment and emotion,' he said, 'and that is why women are generally more receptive to it than men. A scientist in particular should free himself from such a hodge-podge of rituals from another era, since his time is too precious to waste on things in which reason plays practically no part. . . .'

"A year ago such thoughts simply made me smile and shrug my shoulders. But now they have taken on a new significance, one that I would never even have suspected before. I have become much more receptive to them because they express what I myself am experiencing now. And the crux of the matter is that I must come to a decision. I feel that I cannot remain in this situation, since it would quickly turn into hypocrisy. Since religion has no longer any place in my everyday life, I must act accordingly and become somewhat like the insect that, after its slow-moving existence as a chrysalis, undergoes a complete change when it emerges from its dried-up cocoon. . . .

"But if I do this, I'm afraid of causing my wife great pain; it would wound her deeply to see me become a stranger to the faith she believes in so ardently. That's what's worrying me most. I haven't said anything to her yet, but I feel that I must make up my mind soon. And that is part of the reason I'm writing to you, who have always been my friend, to help me to see myself more clearly and to make my wife understand that it's a question of our loyalty to each other, for I can no longer lead this double life, one real and the other a mere pretense. . . ."

The Problem

I think that the crisis in my young friend's life is to some degree that of our modern age as a whole. It is a crisis provoked by the disharmony that results from the sudden growth of scientific research, full of exciting promises on the one hand, and the immobility of a traditional religious outlook on the other. Some will say that it's only a simple difficulty due to growth. But there may be more to it than that. Is it due perhaps to the impossibility of welding two lives, one as demanding as the other, into a unit that is superior to both? Is such a reconciliation possible? And if it is, how are we to achieve it? That is the problem posed by my friend's crisis of conscience. As a first step toward finding the solution we must look at the question as a whole. This is what we intend to do in this book.

I must say immediately that when I speak about a reconciliation, it should not be taken to mean a kind of superficial union between science and faith, an oversimplified attempt at finding scientific data in the truths of faith or, inversely, looking to science to provide confirmation of the faith. This would not be a fusion but merely a "confusion" of the two disciplines. No, it is not a question of an agreement between the two domains on the level of their ideological contents or, as a philosopher would say, their respective objects. Each has its own irreducible character because it draws sustenance from sources proper to itself, and because each corresponds to very different aspects of man's being. Rather it is a question of a concrete reconciliation between two vital needs of the inner life in the very mind and heart of one and the same individual.

Let us also make it clear at once that such an attempt at reconciliation is by no means unusual. The same problem occurs in other domains, but obviously on a different scale. We must not forget that man achieves unity only out of an extraordinary inner complexity, demonstrated by very different levels of activity (intellectual life, emotions, feelings, professional life, sports, etc.). The important thing therefore is not to destroy these varied aspects of his being under the pretext of bringing more unity into his life. That would result in a strange impoverishment indeed. Instead, we must find a unifying principle that can be a source of collaboration, convergence, and mutual support between these diverse activities, always with the intention of insuring the full development of the human personality. It is in this psychological context that our problem occurs—how to unite in one and the same person an authentic life of scientific research and a just as real life of religious belief.

Solutions

Obviously, there are several ways of solving the problem. During the period of open conflict between science and faith there was apparently only one possible answer. It was at best a lazy solution, and it has become less and less acceptable to men of the twentieth century. Essentially it consisted in a careful separation of the two lives in the vain hope of thus avoiding any conflict between them. In fact, it was a renunciation of any hope of achieving a living union between the two spheres of action, that of the scientist and that of the believer. Yet despite its obvious childishness, this was the solution that many scientists of the last century chose when, unwilling to give up their traditional faith, they practiced it on the fringes of their scientific lives, as it were. To their way of thinking, there should be no communication between the oratory and the laboratory. However, when we examine their solution we see that it really is not an answer at all. Basically it is simply burying one's head in the sand and refusing to look at the problem.

In practice this solution results in a paralysis of one of these disciplines. Generally it is the life of religion that will have to pay the penalty because the division is unnatural and contrary to the instinct that urges man, as it does every living being, to maintain within himself a union of life and action. Hence the appeal of the second solution.

The second answer is at once more radical and more tempting: simply suppress one of the two lives and then there is no problem anymore, at least in appearance. That was the solution that occurred spontaneously to my friend when he was confronted with the difficulty—suppress the life of faith. Other believers, on the contrary, take a similar attitude toward the life of science and technical advance. They reject them as incarnations of evil. They dream of a return to a simpler, more primitive life, thus giving some substance to Marxist accusations against religion. Only a few years ago, such believers could write: "Science in our day has passed the stage of ideological conflict with Christianity, but only to take shape again in political and social forms that oppose the Church and seek to kill it." [1]

A strictly rational mind cannot be satisfied with either of these two solutions, or rather with the blind-alley into which they lead, because suppressing one of the elements of a problem has never been the best or even an adequate way of solving it.

[1] *Dieu-Vivant*, No. 7, pp. 12-13.

Moreover, if we wish to approach the question properly we must start with two positive facts and recognize their full significance: first, the existence of science with its present-day progress, its outlook for the future and its ever-spreading influence; and second, the existence of religion, whose adherents demonstrate and practice it in varying degrees, but which, like science, is of such a nature that it demands total dedication.

In examining and understanding these two facts with a view to uniting them in an individual life, we must have the honesty not to caricature either of them. We should neither equate science with the narrow specialist showing no interest in the complexity of reality outside his particular field, nor picture religion as the hidebound devotion of those who confine themselves to a routine practice of their faith. We must begin with data that we accept in all its fullness and richness. It is in this perspective that we wish to find a Christian solution to our problem.

Plan of the Book

Consequently, no one should expect to find in these pages a tract on apologetics, that is, an attempt to defend religion or to prove to unbelievers that it is good. Our aim is more modest, namely, to help the believer who is also a scientist to unify his life through a better understanding of the twofold stream that nourishes him. In order to do this, we must set down both the problem as a whole and its Christian solution, clearly yet systematically, so as not to omit anything essential.

A quick glance over the project will help us to avoid losing sight of the general aim of our undertaking amid the maze of special problems that will arise as we go along.

We shall proceed in two stages. The first stage will deal with the *conditions* under which we must try to unify the two disciplines. This stage will closely examine the main human values involved in the enterprise. Unless we reach a proper understanding of these values we shall run the risk of merely putting a superficial veneer of one discipline upon the other. The second stage will deal with the actual "achievement" of our aim. While we ourselves must exert every effort to succeed, God is still the principal agent. That is why this second part will describe the means that the believing scientist can use to find God.

The contents of the various chapters are as follows.

In Part One, "The Conditions for Unity," the first chapter will carefully define the elements of the problem in all their complexity by specifying the basic psychology of the methods proper to science and faith. This is necessary because we must know whether or not the two viewpoints are compatible before we proceed.

The second chapter will deal with the great dividing line that runs through the universe, separating the world of matter from the world of spirit. Since the Christian solution to the problem is a spiritual one while the scientist is in great part concerned with matter, we must know what is involved when we speak about *matter* and *spirit;* we must be clear about their boundaries and also about the areas in which they can overlap.

Here, and in the following chapter, we must tackle boldly those problems that lie on the borderline between faith and science: materialism, evolution, the possibility that science will synthesize life, the relationship between the brain and thought (as well as the possibilities held out by cybernetics). These problems have often been badly stated since the last century; indeed, such misstatements are still a hindrance to us. They are somewhat like a badly constructed drilling rig which must be rebuilt from the ground up before it will function properly.

The third chapter deals first with the questions raised by the phenomenon of life and its place in the duality of matter and spirit; this in turn leads to the strictly human problem of free will and determinism. When we know to what extent our psychological processes are conditioned by physical, biological and social factors, we can ask what free will is.

On the other hand, it will also be useful to reflect on free will's role in the moral sphere. Does it make man the absolute creator of his destiny, the creator of values which science cannot ignore, as some modern existentialist thinkers believe? Or does it point to a nature that precedes its exercise as a prior, given fact? In short, must science concern itself with the moral problem of human destiny? And in solving this problem, should science and faith compete with each other, or are they instead meant to work together, and how can they do so?

Part Two, "Achieving Unity," begins with the fourth chapter, expounding the classical teaching of finding God in the universe. We start with the mystery of creation, the basic source of the unity that we are seeking, and then we try to ascertain how the scientist can use his work to nourish his spiritual and religious life. A better understanding of God's designs for men in the universe will allow us to start elaborating a theology of work, principally from the scientific point of view.

But only in the fifth chapter does our perspective reach its full range and precision. There we deal with the great biblical teaching on the cosmic role of Christ. In bringing salvation to men, he also gave the universe a new appearance. Our Lord is no stranger to the material world, the world of creation. That is the meaning of the beginning of St. John's Gospel. We shall also see how regrettable it would be to limit the scientist's encounter with God to a purely natural religion, as is too often done. Christianity is a source of life powerful enough to reach to the heart of our problem and provide the true solution that we are seeking.

Thus, the believing scientist must find in the Church, which is the living Christ, the great source of that unity which he seeks. He will do this by being effectively incorporated into the life of charity that animates the Church, and by making his own contribution to that life. His best way of achieving this incorporation will be to understand the Church better, under her various aspects, by ridding himself of many ingrained prejudices. Then, when he sees more clearly that the Church has been the great means of salvation throughout human history, he will find in her the pledge of his meeting with the one God, God the Creator, who revealed himself to us in his Son.

Finally, we see in the sixth chapter a concrete example of a Christian scientist who achieved unity in his life, namely, Father Teilhard de Chardin. There is a summary of his thought and some suggestions for a meaningful approach to his writings. The fact that these have spread so rapidly throughout the world testifies to the profound longing which our contemporaries feel for a real union between science and faith.

In our conclusion we consider how the virtue of hope, the virtue of the Christian committed to temporal affairs, will allow us to grasp more fully the fact that the Christian scientist sees that he is being offered a sublime vocation. While cherishing the hopes that the progress of science offers, he knows that he must nurture in himself a higher hope. Far from destroying the other hopes, it will really guarantee their fulfillment and will demonstrate by its vitality that a fully unified life is indeed possible.

PART ONE
THE CONDITIONS FOR UNITY

I
THE ELEMENTS
OF THE PROBLEM

Scope and Pertinence of the Problem

The search for a union between science and religion is not a new one, but has long been conducted in various forms. In fact, since the breakup of cultural and political unity in the Middle Ages, the relationship between science and religion underwent many vicissitudes before emerging as open conflict in the last century with the advent of positivism and scientism. This conflict died down or at least lost much of its edge when scientism declined in prestige. However, the enmity had affected only limited areas of opinion and had developed principally on the ideological plane, mainly in the form of disputes between intellectuals.

In our day, the problem has not only taken another turn altogether, but has also assumed larger proportions. Even granting that the quarrels of the last century left their mark, we are now confronted less with a doctrinal conflict than with an established divorce between science and religion that tends toward a progressive elimination of religion by science. Generally speaking, this situation is not the outcome of any conscious and concerted effort on the part of the scientific world. It appears to be the inevitable dialectic product of an evolution that is often a matter of regret to those responsible for it.

If, then, we wish to grasp the elements of the problem, we must understand them, not in the context of two adversaries in open

12

conflict, but as part of the development of a historical situation that has as its source the scientific revolution now taking place around us and in which science, by a sort of progressive invasion, seems to be driving before it the forms of thought and life that are foreign to it, such as those of religion.

Hence, in order to define the elements of the problem, we must not regard science and faith as two antagonists facing each other. Rather we should first realize the dynamic role played by science in the divorce of the two disciplines, and the repercussions of the present scientific revolution upon religious life. Then we must take into account the basic nature and demands of the Christian Faith by emphasizing certain of its characteristics that are often misunderstood and that even the faithful themselves have frequently forgotten, thus aiding and abetting the segregation of science from religion.

I. THE SCIENTIFIC REVOLUTION AND ITS REPERCUSSIONS

It has become commonplace to speak about the large and ever-increasing part that science is playing in the world in which we live. In fact, science has become embedded in the very fiber of our civilization and we have become so accustomed to its presence that we forget that this, one of the most important revolutions recorded in the history of mankind, has happened only very recently.

Since this revolution is at the very root of the divorce of science from religion, we shall endeavor to be very clear as to its precise nature, examining its various aspects and, above all, analyzing its effects on present-day religious life.

1. Why Call It a Revolution?

(a) Acceleration of Scientific Progress

When we look at the recent past we are immediately struck by the fact that, in just a few decades, traditional things men used and ways people acted have disappeared in the wake of the upheavals introduced by scientific progress. We see that the old frameworks of thought and practice are being shattered and that we are living in a new age, one which science is beginning to control almost unopposed. After countless centuries of quasi-stagnation, scientific progress has accelerated to a rhythm that is out of all proportion to its slow advance in the past.

(b) A New Vision of the World

One of the most spectacular features of modern scientific progress is the complete change it has wrought in our view of the world by extending our vision in two directions—toward the unimaginably great (the discovery of the structure of the universe) and toward the infinitesimally small (the exploration of the secrets of matter by nuclear science). In fact, this expansion is so great that the numbers it deals in no longer have any meaning for us, so stunned are we by the scope of the vistas laid open before us. Moreover, science now forces us to renounce many familiar convictions that we thought had been settled once and for all (for example, by the discovery of non-Euclidean geometries, the rejection of an absolute time in favor of relativity, the doubt cast on traditional determinism, etc.). Confronted with this new spectacle revealed by science, man feels lost, exiled, driven out of his old world and his accustomed surroundings.

(c) Socialization of Science

Formerly, science was mainly restricted to a small group whom the common man admired but whom he also regarded as being somewhat eccentric, or even out of touch with reality. Researchers were often solitary souls, receiving little or no help from official agencies. (Remember the lamentable conditions in which the Curies had to work!) Scientific research was the domain of the "amateur," while the attention of the public was focused elsewhere, primarily on the Industrial Revolution then taking place.[1]

---

[1] It is true that the Industrial Revolution, brought about as it was by the introduction of machinery, was the result of scientific progress, particularly the discovery of the steam engine. But science was only in its infancy compared to the phenomenal growth it was to have in the twentieth century.

On the contrary, the development of modern science has been made possible only through an ever closer collaboration between researchers working as teams, a socialization of science demanded by the growth of specialization. As the different branches of scientific knowledge advanced, they became extremely diversified; yet at the same time they dovetailed tightly with each other and led inevitably to very close collaboration between specialists (for example, at the atomic level, physics and chemistry lose their boundaries, as will soon be the case with biology, too). In fact, if a modern researcher wants to get results, he must call upon other specialists and study the pertinent scientific literature in innumerable specialized periodicals of many languages. Thus, the control of atomic energy has been made possible only by the combined efforts of scientists from every nation—Americans, Germans, Japanese, English, French, Russians, and others—all basing their work on Einstein's revolutionary concept of the relationship between energy and mass. Planning and building a modern accelerator of particles, such as a synchrotron, calls for an army of specialists and is at the same time of great interest to very many different types of researchers. Science is now a great social and international phenomenon and consequently an important factor is bringing men together.

(d) Science, a Decisive Factor in Power

But modern science also enjoys great prestige and wields a decisive influence among our contemporaries because it has increased to a fantastic degree the power at man's disposal. In particular, since it has learned how to harness primordial energy, the basic energy in matter found in the atomic nucleus, science has given man limitless possibilities of power for mastering the world and conquering the universe. Inexorably led on by the hopes that it has begotten, modern science is no longer confined to the laboratories but engages directly in the practical applications of its discoveries, with the confidence of reaping even more spectacular harvests. The difference between pure and applied science is growing smaller every day as a result of increasing interplay between them, to the point where such a thing as pure, theoretical science may no longer exist.

Science was once, as we have said, a private matter; but due to its emergence as a power factor it has become in modern times one of the most important of public concerns. Nowadays scientific research demands material resources so vast that it can no longer depend on haphazard contributions from philanthropic sources, but must be supported by the State. And the State is only too happy to oblige because of the political and military consequences of research, even though these do not always please the researchers.

Thus, by an inescapable dialectic this process gathers momentum. Scientific research utilizes ever larger groups of people and increasingly greater amounts of material, until ultimately whole countries are concerned with it. The layman often sees only the immediate benefits he derives from scientific research: a more comfortable way of life, labor-saving electrical appliances in the home, audio-visual devices, faster travel, and the like. He does not see that the stakes are much higher, that mankind's very future is in the balance.

(e) Science Makes Man Face His Destiny

This is what makes science so awe-inspiring, and this too explains the tragic dilemma posed by science. It gives men such great power that they are driven to ask themselves the basic question: What should this vast power be used for? In other words, modern science has ushered in a new era marked by responsibility for the very future of all mankind.

This new responsibility was spectacularly demonstrated by a simple event that became a dividing line in history. When, on August 6, 1945, Colonel Tibbets of the U.S. Air Force dropped the bomb on Hiroshima from his B-29, he performed an act that was apparently identical with those of hundreds of his predecessors in the war. The only difference (and what a difference!) was in the bomb. Instead of killing some hundreds or at most some thousands of people, as conventional bombs had hitherto done, this one annihilated 80,000 people in a few seconds, a number that grew in five years to a total of 282,000 dead as a result of the deadly aftereffects of the explosion.

That was the brutal fact that publicly ushered in a new era, the era of a colossal power that men could use for good or evil. That is why we must speak about a new responsibility, one which primarily falls on all those who took part in the discovery and on the politicians who exploit it, but which also devolves upon each one of us whether we like it or not.

In fact, as we must not forget, responsibility in any area grows with the power at one's disposal. Driving a car entails greater obligation than riding a bicycle, and insurance companies, who undertake to assume part of this responsibility, are careful to prorate their premiums according to the type of vehicle being used by their clients.

Further, present-day thermonuclear bombs are much more powerful than the Hiroshima bomb, just as the latter was in relation to the conventional projectiles used during World War II. Hence we can see immediately that the enormous increase of force and energy produced by science involves for all men, and especially their rulers, an increased responsibility that is incomparably greater than that of past generations.

By thus putting at our disposal new possibilities that we can use with equal ease for our ruin or our benefit, science has brought us face to face with the issue, compelling us to choose our own destiny. And this holds true not only for the inorganic sciences; it can be said just as truly about the life sciences such as genetics and embryology, which open up frightening prospects for modifying man's very heredity. We can see why Huxley was able to assert that man "now has conscious control over evolution." That, in our opinion, is the basic reason why scientific research enjoys such great prestige and why it is now endowed with a dignity that its first pioneers did not even dream of.

Finally, science is no longer concerned with man's "terrestrial" life alone, but also with his attitude toward the whole created universe, as a result of the vistas opened up by the new science of astronautics. Here, too, when the layman is confronted with the orbital flights made by American or Russian cosmonauts, he reacts superficially, seeing only the "science fiction" aspect of the matter or regarding it as a kind of political contest, a race for glory, as it were. Of course, it goes without saying that the development of orbital flight has a much deeper significance than all that. Of all the forces of nature that man has tried to tame, gravity is the most fundamental, the most inescapable; the one which, by its continual presence within and around him, recalls him to the irksome reality of his earthly prison. The dream of finally escaping from the earth is as old as humanity itself. And the first man who is able to break the bond of gravity, to escape from this globe on which he was born and to look down on the planet Earth with a certain detachment as if it were a cumbersome body from which he has been released, that man will usher in a new era, an era of freedom, of actual direct access to a kingdom without bounds, the cosmos itself.

These are, in brief, some of the principal features of the revolution responsible for the enormous growth of modern science and for the vital role it has assumed in a civilization which it has permeated and shaped.

2. Effects of Science on Religion

In a partnership between two men it often happens that, while one of them becomes increasingly important to the business, the other is pushed to one side or even completely eliminated. Somewhat the same thing happens in the everyday life of a society in which varied activities must be carried on at different levels. For example, the growth of technology can impose a mode of living which leads to changes in the individual's physical or social life because it upsets the traditional balance and even because it may make certain sociological structures obsolete.

To some extent, that is what has happened to religion (and morality, too) in our day. Like a vigorous plant that grows and spreads so rapidly that it smothers other vegetation, modern science was bound to inhibit other types of human activity, especially those that are of a diametrically different nature, such as traditional religious faith. The process was aided by the nature of things (the individual characteristics of science and religion) as well as by the historical context in which the division took place. By reviewing these factors we can perhaps get an inkling as to whether or not the divorce between science and faith is final and irrevocable.

(a) Differences Encouraging the Break

We can say at once that modern science, in its general outlook and aims, is opposed to religion. Formerly science, as a private matter without any great influence on the outside world, was somewhat "contemplative" in nature. To some extent it shared the strictly religious outlook, so that Newton could remark to Bentley: "When I wrote my Treatise about our System, I had an eye upon such principles as might work with considering men, for the belief of a Deity, and nothing can rejoice me more than to find it useful for that purpose." [2]

But we have seen how modern science, by the very methods it has developed and upon which it thrives, aims at being efficient and producing great results. Hence, even though scientists may wish to remain "contemplatives," they are caught in a whirlpool from which they cannot escape. They are involved in a chain reaction, which urges men to use science to increase their power; and this increased mastery is used in turn to make science produce new results. In reality, we are confronted here with a sort of intoxication that clouds men's vision and turns their eyes toward other horizons.

This results in a progressive deadening of the spiritual faculties and the decline of the purely interior life; and the climate that is indispensable for religious faith gradually disappears. When we value only the material efficiency developed by science, we inevitably become devoted to purely earthly and material things. Gradually, we become insensitive to the things of God, to the world of the spirit which presupposes above all a personal commitment to God, an interior communion with a reality that is perceived mainly in the silence of the heart. But all of this is very foreign to the world which the scientific revolution has shaped.

Another characteristic of science similar to the foregoing encourages the divorce between the two worlds. Modern science, an affair of pure reason devoted to the absolute control of matter, accustoms man to attacking every problem with the conviction that he can solve it with his brain and his machines alone. Therefore

[2] *Isaaci Newtoni opera quae exstant,* Commentariis illustrabat Samuel Horsley, excudebat J. Nichols, (Londini, 1779-85), Vol. IV, p. 429.

science, discarding the idea that any kind of mystery, either metaphysical or religious, can exist, relies solely upon itself. Thus it apparently makes futile the practice of having recourse to God to obtain light and strength from him.[3]

We can easily understand how the believing scientist may experience some difficulty in retaining the conviction that primacy must be given to spiritual values. But what happens to the man in the street, who is affected by and even welcomes the pervasive influence of scientific progress without thinking much about it, who is immersed in an atmosphere that is no longer the climate of faith in which his forefathers lived? The fact is that many observers have noted the decline of religion wherever a scientifically and technically advanced civilization has developed. This can perhaps explain the pessimistic reaction of some believers toward scientific developments. Certainly, there are many scientists who do not allow science to exercise an adverse effect on their religious principles and lives. But despite the good faith of these men, the repercussions of science on religion seem to be due not to the data of science itself, but to the special outlook fostered by the progress of science. The whole problem, then, is to know whether this conflict of outlook between religion and science is surmountable or not; and that is the aim of the pages that follow.

(b) History Has Promoted the Division

However, we must not think that science alone is responsible for the divorce. Science did play the most dynamic role in it, but it is no less true to say that if many believers had perhaps practiced their faith with more intelligence and sincerity, science would not have pushed it aside so easily. In fact, historians of the recent past have been able to paint a faithful and not very flattering picture of religion at grips with the scientific revolution, a revolution that

---

[3] Another friend of mine, a meteorologist, told me that he was convinced that the phenomena producing the weather are rigorously determined, although we cannot yet formulate very precise laws for the way they work. As a result, he had difficulty in understanding why the Church now, in the middle of the twentieth century, could still order prayers to be said to change the weather, to get rain or sunshine, seeing that the result had already been decided by an inexorable process. But my friend forgot that prayer, far from interrupting a predetermined set of events, has been included by God in his providential plan that knows neither past nor future.

took over the territory it invaded only because it found it more or less unoccupied. Moreover, the Marxists and positivists were only too ready to exploit science and involve it in their plans to banish religion.

We must first acknowledge that, unhappily, the rapid growth of science was not matched by an equally swift growth in faith, which often remained childish.

This difference in growth rate is the result of historical developments that are too lengthy to describe in detail here—nor is this the place for it—but whose general outlines are as follows:

During the Middle Ages, religion permeated all of social life and civilization because they were centered on God and on man's relationship with him. But the mark of modern times, beginning with the Renaissance, is the displacement of God and religion. Man and his mastery of this world have now become the principal focus of interest. This process of laicization, of "secularization," took place slowly. Under the monarchical political regimes, official institutions remained Christian, and the Church still played a leading role; yet she was often used as a screen for underhanded political maneuvers. But despite the apparent ascendancy of religion, science made considerable gains over faith, which felt sure of itself because it was protected by the ruling political powers.

The decay of the old order inevitably revealed the divorce of science from religion among the intellectuals of Europe, a split which encouraged the development of the same process on the popular level when science reached its revolutionary stage. Too few Christians at that time possessed the clarity of vision to assess the situation. When the labor question came up, with few exceptions they were deaf to the pope's appeals for effective action and left the attempt to find a solution to the proponents of Marxist socialism.[4]

We may well fear that the same thing will happen if religious men stand aside while science is building the modern world, and if they do not effectively show that their faith is not childish, but strong and mature.

Many Christians really deserve to be called childish because of the way they react to science. Every important scientific discovery,

---

[4] See the words of Pius XI on the grave scandal of the loss of the working classes by the Church in the nineteenth century.

particularly if it is at all spectacular, makes them more uneasy because they think that science is gradually disproving and supplanting the religious explanation of the universe.

As we shall see more fully in the fourth chapter, their uneasiness comes from their conception of God as the great mysterious force of nature, which is the only explanation of everything in a world that is still humanly unknowable or inexplicable. Thus, for example, they regard the mystery-shrouded origins of life as a subject which must always elude the scientist. And, they say, even if the scientist does come close to the discovery, there will always be an unexplainable element left, the final sanctuary of the Creator's mysterious workings.

This vaguely naturalistic concept reduces God's action to the same level as created activity, yet it naively tries to preserve the inviolable character of his operations by insisting that, in the last analysis, man can never unveil them. This is a gross error because it thinks of God in human terms, denying in practice the transcendental and analogical aspect of his operations. Then, too, such a reaction against scientific progress is partly the result of a pessimistic view of the world which regards matter as the chosen ground of some evil principle, an outlook that is really only a type of undeclared dualism holding that the life of faith should develop only as a kind of disembodied spirituality.[5] Every victory by science is therefore regarded as a triumph of matter over spirit, of evil over good. According to this pseudo-Christian viewpoint, whose popularity even today we must not try to hide, scientific progress has gradually eliminated God from the world. This theory seems to offer an explanation for the consequences of the scientific revolution as they affect religion: but be that as it may, it does promote the divorce between science and religion.

In practice, people who hold this opinion react to science by following a policy of withdrawing from everyday life and from the

[5] The Church has repeatedly stressed the need for bringing spiritual principles to bear on everyday life and has continually warned us not to underestimate the contribution that technology can make in achieving that end. The Holy See's main pronouncements on this subject have been collected in F. Russo's *Technique et Conscience religieuse* (Bonne Presse, 1961).

mainstream of history, a policy which they use to justify their "absenteeism." Because they insist on regarding the kingdom of heaven as existing only in the next life,[6] they have forgotten that the kingdom began on earth and must be built up by our efforts here below.

It is obvious that, with the ground so well prepared, the positivism of the last century had a golden opportunity to sow in men's minds the idea that religion was only a stage of historical development which they had outgrown and which had to give way before the advance of science. This idea, the main tenet of present-day rationalism, has been well expressed by Bertrand Russell: "The unyielding rationalist has a better faith and a more unbending optimism than any of the timid seekers after the childish comforts of a less adult age." [7]

Marxism then took over the idea from positivism and formulated a critique of religion, depicting it as a mere illusion of happiness, a mirage that prevented men from attaining the only real human happiness, which was to be ushered in by modern science and technology. Consequently, when a Christian is confronted with the energetic striving for improvement that is so characteristic of the modern world, he must be particularly on his guard because he runs the risk of appearing like mankind's poor relation, ineffective and completely out of touch, thus giving substance to the Marxist's contemptuous view of religion. And actually, because many believers do look back nostalgically to "the good old days," they seem to be strangers in the new world which science has built without any help from them. By resigning themselves to this role, they confirm the low opinion that modern atheists, following Nietzsche, have of them: "The Christian is useless, out of touch and without spirit; he is a stranger to the work of the world." [8]

The tragedy is that here as in so many other areas, such as the quest for a solution to the social problem, the Christian's faith provides him with all he needs to play a bigger part than anyone

---

[6] Whole generations of Christians have been taught from childhood to sing hymns that look to the next life alone.

[7] B. Russell, *The Scientific Outlook* (New York, W. W. Norton & Company, Inc., 1931), p. 133.

[8] F. Nietzsche, *Volonté de puissance* (Wurzbach), p. 152.

else in building the modern world. Sad to say, many do not see this and leave their talents unused. However, the criticism by positivist and Marxist atheism has gone far toward awakening in Catholic circles a healthy reaction to this isolationism.[9] When we study the scriptures and the lessons of classical theology, we can see that the criticism levelled against Christians is justified by the way so many of them have forgotten the true dimensions of their faith. Going back to these primary sources, we shall, in chapters four and five of this book, try to outline a Christian solution to the problem of combining a religious life with a life of science. Before we do this, however, it will be helpful if we examine the precise meaning of faith and its exact nature, as contrasted with the attitude proper to science.

II. RELIGIOUS FAITH

Without anticipating the second part of this book, let us briefly review the place of faith in human life. This will allow us to see more clearly the relationship of faith to scientific knowledge.

1. Origin of Faith

Man, God's creature, can find his true development, his full happiness only by living in union with his Creator through knowledge and love. Thus, even from the point of view of our very nature, God is the real goal of human life, our reason for existing. We are made for him. While this holds true for all creatures, our orientation toward God can and should be conscious and free, for it is the foundation of all morality and religion. We shall discuss the psychological proofs of this statement later, in chapter three.

Now, as men we cannot fully know God, who is Absolute Being,

[9] F. Russo gives a good historical summary in his article "Cent années d'un dialogue difficile entre la science et la foi (1850-1950)" in the volume *Pensée scientifique et Foi chrétienne* (Recherches et débats, Paris, Fayard, 1953), pp. 7-30.

a hidden God, a pure spirit. That is the tragedy and the greatness of our human condition: we have been made for God; but God, by his very nature, is hidden from us because our knowledge is concerned with tangible things, the objects of science. Nevertheless, since the concrete realities that go to make up nature are the created work of God, the Creator shows himself to some extent through the world around us. It should therefore be easy for us to find God in his works.

Unfortunately, however, this search for God is difficult and hazardous because we are inclined to see only creatures instead of using them as stepping stones to the Creator; and we cannot find in creatures the joy for which we are made. This is the result of sin, of our human wretchedness, our inborn weakness, particularly our pride, and our spiritual blindness. These would bring us up against a blank wall if God had not taken the initiative by giving us a means of deliverance and salvation.

Because finding God in creatures is difficult and full of pitfalls, and because he is, nevertheless, the sole aim of human life, he has revealed himself more clearly in his Son. By taking on human nature, Christ placed God within man's reach. He is thus the great revelation of God to men, and he brings salvation to them by offering them the opportunity of partaking of God's own life.

Finding God through his works is possible but difficult. It can be accomplished by an act of purely natural reasoning, by going from the work to the author of the work. This in itself is not an act of faith but rather of rational thought; it leads, however, to a merely external and analogical knowledge of God.

On the other hand, finding God in his revelation through Christ cannot be the result of a reasoning process. It is instead an act of trust in a Word expressed as an actual Person, the Person of Christ. It is the act of faith properly so called that leads to a personal encounter with God. Then he is no longer reached through a reasoning process but as the result of an act of divine love, a personal gift from God to man. And this encounter assumes the characteristics of a liberation, a happy salvation. It has an existential quality about it and takes the form of an intimately experienced knowledge of God's divinity.

2. Is Faith Irrational?

Obviously, faith is not rational in origin or motivation because it is not the result of reasoning but of God's action upon man; it is a meeting between the soul and God which should lead to divine love's breaking down the barriers of sin.

But let us examine the matter more closely. First of all, reason has a part to play before the act of faith. Its part comes at the stage which theologians call the preparation for faith, that is, in a reasoned assessment of the signs by which God guarantees his revelation. In this respect and from the psychological point of view, the act of religious faith is not one without possible parallels in similar human acts. Thus, when I take a friend's word for something which I cannot verify for myself, I make an act of human faith. I believe something, not because I see the evidence for it, but because I judge that my friend is trustworthy. Then my reason intervenes, not to grasp the internal truth of the thing reported—for I cannot verify that—but to weigh the reasons for the confidence I have in my friend. This is called a judgment or assessment of credibility.

When we think about it, we see that such acts of faith are commonplace in our everyday life, and that we simply could not continue without them. We make acts of implicit faith in regard to the vast majority of those things which we daily take for granted, for we simply could not verify all of them even if we wanted to. Certain branches of knowledge, such as history and geography, are possible only as a result of acts of human faith, as a result of trust in the testimony of those who report the happenings of the past or discover the facts of the present. In purely scientific fields, continual acts of faith are required, for if every specialist had to verify the findings of every researcher, science would be impossible. So true is this that we can say that science makes progress only by first making acts of faith.

Therefore, as regards its psychological and human aspects, an act of religious faith is not at all irrational but is instead a normal way of arriving at truth; and the scientist should not find such an act repugnant. Like Monsieur Jourdain in Molière's *Bourgeois gentilhomme,* who was surprised to find that he had been speaking prose all his life, the scientist makes innumerable acts of faith every day without being aware that he is doing so. The only difference between his acts of faith and those of the believer is that religious faith is the product of a divine action and that it leads to a meeting with a Person, a Father who must be everything to men, giving them salvation by an act of ineffable love. But in its preliminary stage, religious faith respects the workings of reason. Just as the historian assesses the trustworthiness of his sources, or the scientific researcher concludes that he can have confidence in a colleague who testifies that he has carried out such and such an experiment (and we must remember that some experiments are almost impossible to repeat), so too does the believer judge that the signs which God has given as a guarantee of his revelation are genuine and can reasonably be believed.

We stress this point so much because the mistaken idea that religious faith is irrational is firmly rooted in many minds and is fervently preached by Marxists. Faith, therefore, does not dispense with reason in favor of absurdity or condemn it to blind, passive submission. Rather, it is a voluntary allegiance given, under the influence of grace, to a divine love that offers us salvation. And to guarantee the reasonable nature of faith, "The many wonderful external signs God has given . . . are sufficient to prove with certitude by the natural light of reason alone the divine origin of the Christian religion." [10]

The reasonable nature of the act of faith is seen not only in the preparatory steps but also, and especially, in its goal, the meeting with God.

In fact, what is God but the infinitely intelligent Being, pure thought absolutely intelligible in itself? Hence when the believer accepts God's revelation by faith, he knows that his act does not lead him out into the darkness of the irrational, the absurd, but toward an intelligence that is the source of all thought, of all the laws of the universe, the fountainhead of all intelligibility.

At this point we must be clear about the concept of mystery in religion. The term "dogma" simply means the knowledge about salvation which has been revealed to us and which is accepted by

[10] Pius XII, Encyclical *Humani generis* (Glen Rock, N. J., Paulist Press, 1950), n. 4.

faith. Yet the word is often given a meaning that tends to confuse people; it is taken to mean a statement without proof, a prejudice, a kind of sacred cow that must not be disturbed or prodded by an investigator. This is the sense in which we take the word when we speak of dogmatism; and this is the only sense in which the positivist or Marxist uses it when he is attacking religion.

Religious dogma is something completely different; it means the mysteries of religion that are reached by faith. But why are there mysteries in religion? For the very simple reason that God's inner nature eludes all investigation by the human mind. Hence, a mystery in the religious sense means something that is unknowable, not in itself, but by our finite minds. These, because they are created, are limited and restricted in what they can do, and they cannot claim to be able to comprehend an object that is immeasurably beyond them. Even the scientist encounters the fact of mystery in his work; that is, he finds things that he knows are intelligible but that evade his best efforts to form concepts of them. So, shortly before his death, Henry Poincaré was able to say: "Scientists are trained to solve mysteries, but of course they always end up by finding more mysteries a little further on!" If our minds have so much difficulty in solving the mysteries of the material world, how powerless they are when confronted with their Creator, a pure spirit beyond the scope of our imagination!

Some may object and ask what is the good of revealing God's mysteries, because even then they will still be unknowable and therefore unusable. But it is the very function of revelation to give us some knowledge of the divine life by means of, and despite, the mysteries it involves. We have to live our lives and find our salvation by partaking of the divine life, and so we can readily see why God must come to us by revealing some of the riches of his own life. Here we rediscover the original, biblical meaning of the word "mystery," a meaning too often forgotten in oversimplified, childish formulations of the Christian faith.

In the biblical sense, a mystery is to be defined not so much in terms of something unknowable as in the sense of a partial unveiling or revealing (revelation) of the divine life. A mystery, far from signifying something that is hidden completely, irrevocably, and forever, means something that is unveiled for man by faith. Hence it does not imply impenetrability or inaccessibility; rather it is something that can enlighten and nourish the believer's mind and soul. Concretely and basically, the central mystery (for St. Paul, for example) is Christ himself coming to bring us salvation by admitting us to participation in God's own life. It is true, of course, that faith does not eliminate the basic disproportion between a created intelligence and God's pure, absolute thought; but it does allow us to approach that thought in a manner adapted to our capabilities while we await the full, beatific vision of God in heaven. Yet even in heaven our minds, although filled to capacity with the sight of God, will never be able to understand fully the infinite riches of the mystery that is God.

Perhaps some parallel examples may help us here. The human eye cannot look at the sun because it is too bright for direct vision and repels, as it were, any such attempt at contact with it. This does not mean that the sun is not visible, but rather that it is too much so. If we had no way of shading our eyes so that we could gaze at the sun itself, we would perhaps regard its light as something mysterious, beyond our capacity to understand, but we could not conclude that the sun was unknowable in itself.

Take another example. The theories of a scientific genius like Einstein are beyond the reach of the man in the street who knows nothing about higher mathematics and frankly confesses that such things are mysteries to him. But when this ordinary man sees Einstein's theories being used to produce spectacular effects like the atomic bomb, he is filled with admiration for the profundity of the scientist's thought and accepts it with all the firmness of an act of faith. Perhaps he believes more firmly in relativity on this basis than if, unaware of Einstein's greatness, he had painfully tried to master the theory himself. Considering the inadequacy of the means at his disposal and the disproportion between his ability and Einstein's genius, his own personal search for internal evidence and his attempt to understand the theory as such would perhaps not have given him the same firm faith he now possesses.

Therefore, although the act of faith does not provide intrinsic evidence (and this is as true of religious faith as of the human faith that plays so great a part in our daily lives), it does give a conviction, a certitude that is all the firmer the greater the authority of him in whom we believe. Accordingly, a truck driver's faith can be as great as—and even firmer and hence more reasonable than—a theologian's. When the man in the street believes in relativity, even though it involves things that may seem very strange to him, he believes in it because he has profound esteem for its author. His faith is reasonable and not illogical, because he knows that Einstein was convinced of the validity of the theory, and he puts his faith in the great man's genius, trusting him completely. Psychologically speaking, the religious man does somewhat the same thing. He knows that God is perfect, that he is pure intellect and love personified; hence, knowing that God cannot deceive him and lead him into error, he has the profoundest faith in him. Therefore, he believes most firmly in every revealed truth, however mysterious, because he knows that in God's sight this truth is not a mystery but as clear as day. Hence his faith, based as it is upon the supreme authority of God, is not unreasonable or illogical. The only difference between this example and the preceding one is that in religious faith God is not only the motive for faith but also its original cause, by reason of the enlightenment of grace. As a matter of fact, the object of this religious faith is not an abstract truth or something foreign to ordinary everyday life but a Person, a loving Father, revealing himself to his children.

3. Science and Faith

We can now understand better the basic difference between science and faith, as well as the common bond between them.

(a) On Different Levels

Science is a reasoned effort to understand the world around us. It is concerned with discovering the laws that govern and the relationships that exist between the various material and psychical phenomena of the universe. It evolves theories expressing men's attempts to synthesize the greatest possible number of facts, and while trying to master the secrets of nature, it learns how to harness the energies found in nature. It develops and makes progress by striving to understand the inner nature of reality. Yet, as we have seen, it can exist only through close collaboration between the specialists in its various branches, each relying on the others, trusting them and accepting their conclusions. Nowadays, no genius, however great, can learn the specialized findings of every department of science: a whole lifetime would not be sufficient for that. So, when working at a level that uses the results of the various specialties, each scientist must trust the others and believe the results of their research. Therefore, since a comprehensive knowledge of science is not possible at this level, the scientist must rely to a great extent on data that he accepts solely on scientific faith.

Nevertheless, at the level of each particular science, the scientific method eliminates as far as possible the argument from authority and strives to give each scientist an absolutely clear and mathematically certain knowledge of his specialty.

Religious faith has a totally different aim. As Paul Ricoeur says: "The world of science is necessarily constructed outside the area in which anyone or anything can be damned or saved." [11] This area is the domain of faith, which seeks an encounter with a Person, with divine love. The most familiar analogy used to explain religious faith is the confidence that two people in love have in each other. The trust that nourishes this human faith is hard to express, for it involves the indescribably personal meeting of two souls. It is not a question of finding an explanation for something; rather it is the communing of two persons with each other. Although the psychological development of the lover's faith in his beloved follows somewhat the same process as the scientist's faith in his colleagues, the lover's faith is different in its approach and its flowering because it is essentially a dynamic, voluntary involvement with another person.

Thus the lover knows his loved one in his own love, in the trust that he lavishes upon her. He knows that he can reasonably depend on her word (in fact, he often makes up arguments to justify what she says or does). But, at least in the beginning, he spends little time analyzing the nature of the attraction she has for him or the real motives of mind and heart behind her personality and actions. The essential thing is that he finds her utterly charming

---

[11] Russo, *op. cit.*, p. 81.

and attractive just as she is, an alluringly vital yet psychologically mysterious creature.

It is somewhat the same in the case of the average believer. The essential thing for him is his meeting with God, the source of all joy and salvation. His trust in God is not blind, because he knows that he can place the greatest confidence in the Being in whom he believes and to whom he gives his allegiance. It is of small consequence to him that the mystery through which he attains God says nothing to his mind. He knows that, far from being absurd or irrational, this mystery of dogma presupposes in its very formulation an intelligibility of the highest degree, and he is satisfied with that knowledge.

We can see then that while science and faith have certain common characteristics in their psychological development, they still operate on two very different levels. Therefore there can never be any real rivalry, much less opposition, between them, because before two things can be opposed to each other they must be able to confront one another on the same ground. Someone may object that although faith has a structure different from that of science, it does nevertheless assert certain truths, sometimes contradicting science thereby. But even when this happens, faith is not speaking from the same point of view as science. "Faith gives us 'eyes' to see the same universe [that science sees], not however as if we had been given a sixth sense to perceive new properties in objects, but to unravel the meaning, the significance, the basic orientation of this same universe where scientific research is pursued on its own level. Properly speaking, faith does not offer us new objects of knowledge but only a sign, an indication of a new realm of truth to which an object belongs; it gives us a supernatural knowledge which, on a strictly human level, neither adds nor subtracts anything from the natural knowledge that we can have of the same object." [12]

(b) A Common Source

Despite the different postures of science and faith, we can point to another aspect of the connection between them, an aspect which

[12] Russo, *op. cit.*, Article by P. Germain, p. 109.

we shall deal with in greater detail in future chapters and which lays the foundations for the union that we seek—the *common source* of the two disciplines, God himself.

Science studies nature, creation, which is the work of God. Faith is a direct, personal encounter with the same God, following a different route. But in both cases the goal is the same although it is reached in very dissimilar ways. In science, we proceed by reasoning and study from the work to the Author of the work, whom we reach from the outside, as it were. By faith, we reach him in a personal communion that starts from his direct intervention, his own revelation of his inner life.

Perhaps another example will help us here. Suppose a great artist has finished an important piece of work that contains a spiritual message, a profound meaning, a real testament of genius which we can discover only by analyzing the work. Obviously, the ideal way to find the message would be to interview the artist. Suppose, however, that he has disappeared or cannot be reached, but that he has told his son the meaning of his masterpiece. In that case there are two ways to find out what we want to know. First, we can analyze the work itself by means of comparative research; this is what the scientist does, starting from facts, the object of science. The second way is to have a communication from the artist, a tradition or handing on, a transmission of his thought through his son; this is the way of faith. It is obvious that the two ways cannot contradict each other since both have a common source. If there is a contradiction it can only be an apparent one, either because the investigator is mistaken in what he deduces from the work, or because the believer interprets badly the son's message, which, obviously, will not be expressed in the same form of words as the investigator's scientific deduction.

If we apply this metaphor to our problem—and it is only a metaphor, not to be pushed too far—we are able to see more clearly that faith and science cannot contradict each other in their ideological content. We shall not deal further with this aspect of the question. Later, in chapter five, when speaking about Christ and the Church, we shall seek to gain a better understanding of the assurance that the believer gets from the Church's guarantee that she is handing down unerringly the revealed deposit of faith. This guarantee obliges the believer to give priority to the interpretation provided by the Church, the messenger of Christ, whenever a truth of the Faith appears to contradict a scientific finding. We shall see how we should deal with this problem, and we shall discuss the famous trial of Galileo as a case in point.

Having made this clear and prepared the ground, we shall be in a better position to pursue our aim, ascertaining the way in which one can combine the practice of the Christian faith with a life devoted to science. For, even if we do know that, in theory, science and faith cannot contradict each other, in actual fact the pervasive influence of science and the outlook it fosters oblige us to reassess the truths of faith in their proper dimensions so that we may achieve the mutually beneficial union between the two types of life that we are seeking. We shall be more easily able to cope with this practical problem when we understand the fundamental natures of the different methods that faith and science use, as well as the place each discipline should have when integrated into the rest of life and when the two are functioning as one.

II
MATTER AND SPIRIT

Since, by definition, the life of faith presupposes the existence of another, spiritual world besides the material universe, our first step must be to take account of the reality and meaning of this non-material world. And since material things are directly and easily accessible, because they are the very warp and woof of our everyday lives as well as the object of scientific research and technology, we must try to see if we can use them as stepping stones toward the things of the spirit.

Even though we already have faith, we shall find it useful to make the effort to reflect, so that we may gain a better appreciation of spiritual values, those values which have no appeal to our senses and do not register on our instruments of measurement, but which the religious man regards as even more real than material things. How, then, should we begin our search?

We can start with the following reasoning: the life of religion must be spiritual, that is, not reducible to matter; and if it is not a mere illusion but is really open to us, there must therefore exist in us a part of our being that can be discerned by thought and that belongs to this spiritual order, going beyond the world of matter. Do we human beings possess a center of activity that fulfills these conditions?

We shall not begin from any preconceived idea, but shall proceed only along the most natural line of development. Since the life of religion is a fact, we must first ask: Is this life of religion the product of illusion, or is it, on the contrary, the manifestation of a non-material world?

I. APPROACHING THE WORLD OF THE SPIRIT

There are many avenues of approach to the world in which the life of religion develops. We shall begin with the one that we think is the most ordinary and mundane and the least biased toward the objective we have in mind. This is the approach from knowledge of the material world, which is so familiar to the scientist. Other starting points, such as the knowledge we gain by self-reflection, or our moral life, are also available, and we shall speak about them in the next chapter. But the approach we have chosen here has the advantage of not starting from special qualities which only some individuals possess. Thus, it does not invoke subjective and emotional factors, thereby casting doubt on the objectivity of the result. Nor do we propose to construct a psychological theory; that would bring us too far afield. Instead we shall analyze the simple fact that every human being, child or adult, possesses some knowledge of the material universe. We shall then see clearly whether or not we can find in this typically human act of knowing any indication that men can engage in an activity that is not completely reducible to matter.

Let us make it clear once and for all that we are taking the word "matter" here in its broadest and most ordinary sense, a point that must be stressed because no word lends itself more to ambiguity. In philosophical language, matter often means the substratum of every material being, an indeterminate principle; in scientific language, on the contrary, it is simply one form of a tangible reality that can also be presented under another form, namely energy. Here we use the term in contradistinction to spirit, as meaning *everything that is accessible to our senses or our measuring instruments,* which are the extensions of our senses. Matter, then, for us means whatever can be measured or weighed, whatever we perceive when it impinges on our senses, whatever can be located in time and space, whether it be a simple force field (e.g., electromagnetic force) or a reality as elusive as the most ephemeral of particles (such as the meson).

This concept of matter is of capital importance for a proper understanding of what we are about to say. In fact, if we were to take the word "matter" in the strict scientific sense, we would put ourselves at the disadvantage of giving our inquiry too limited a base, conceding that only science can reach the knowledge we seek. Actually the search is of vital interest to every man in every aspect of his being.

1. Man's Curiosity

One of the most striking characteristics of man is his insatiable curiosity about everything. While animals show interest in other creatures only to satisfy their alimentary or sexual needs, men on the contrary seem to be animated by a spirit that urges them on to take a practical interest in everything. Of course, each individual has his own particular object or field of curiosity, but it is precisely the extraordinary variety of interests found among a group of individuals that shows that men have a truly universal flexibility and capacity for wonder.

This quality is fround to a pre-eminent degree in the true scientist. Starting with an unusual capacity for wonder at the most natural of phenomena, he launches out into scientific research, never satisfied with results and always searching for deeper and wider knowledge.

This flexibility, this looking toward boundless horizons can have only one meaning—that man has dominion over material things. A piece of wax that has received one imprint is not thereby made more receptive to another because, since it is material, its capacity is strictly limited in space and time. Animals do exhibit greater receptivity than inanimate objects but it is largely dependent upon organic urges, almost all of which are the same among members of the same species. Therefore, at this simple level of apprehension, we must presuppose that man has a center of activity that is capable of ever greater receptivity, one that is not passive but dynamic and purposeful, urging him forward in an almost desperate search for knowledge. That is the whole meaning of scientific progress.

2. Need for Explanation

But man does not merely begin to wonder and then do nothing about it. His wondering generally has a precise purpose, that of finding an explanation for a phenomenon that he has observed; he tries to understand what he observes and to incorporate it into what he already knows. A child who has dreamed of owning a particular toy begins to take it apart as soon as he gets it to find out how it is made. By so doing, he is simply exhibiting this typically human tendency in its natural state.

At this stage we see one of the most significant of human characteristics—the compelling need to find a connection between an observed phenomenon and something else. It is as if we can scarcely bring ourselves to accept an observed fact as something completely isolated. We experience a kind of discomfort or uneasiness at its strangeness and are eager to try to connect it with something we already know, that is, to find an explanation for it, as if to reassure ourselves. In fact, our eagerness to accept an oversimplified explanation for some phenomenon has often done a disservice to our thirst for knowledge and the progress that it stimulates, for then we have an illusory sense of satisfaction.[1] But even though laziness or sloppy thinking sometimes makes us accept easy explanations, we still possess and are urged on by this profound human tendency to investigate.

The role of science has consisted especially in refining, channeling and verifying the explanations we have found for various phenomena, thereby both deepening and satisfying our need to know. Whole books have been written about scientific explanation, but this is not the place to hold forth on the subject.[2] Let us simply recall that the advance of science has always aimed at going beyond simple perception mixed with subjective feelings, preferring quantitative measurement to qualitative appreciation. For instance, science defines a color by its wavelength, it transcends superficial appearances (e.g., Copernicus' teaching that the earth revolves around the sun), and it avoids as far as possible the assumption that there are artificial breaks in reality such as those

[1] The history of science shows this process at work in every epoch: first comes an immediate explanation, generally coinciding with appearances (e.g., Ptolemy's plan of the universe); and only later is a more impersonal explanation evolved (e.g., the Copernican system).

[2] See, for example, R. B. Braithwaite's *Scientific Explanation,* (New York, Cambridge University Press, 1953), and E. Meyerson's work, *De l'explication dans les Sciences,* (2 vols., 1921). On this whole question, see also J. Ullmo, *La Pensée scientifique moderne* (Flammarion, 1958).

invoked by unsophisticated empiricism (e.g., it explains the differences of living species by evolution). Its special method of approach is to seek more ways of reaching the true nature of reality by employing operating techniques of a logico-mathematical type that all tend toward the discovery of an ever greater and closer union between the largest possible number of phenomena. For example, general relativity has given a unifying explanation for many facts; and today there is a search for a theory that would correlate electro-magnetism and gravitation.

At present, we are at a stage when matter almost disappears. We are now going beyond primitive sense data (i.e., beyond the stimulation of any one of our senses, such as sight or touch) and are reaching out to other data that are more and more rarefied. We are able to investigate outside the range of our senses by means of detecting devices that our inventive powers have developed. Nowadays, starting with material objects, with measurable, tangible, localized objects, science is able to achieve results that are of a different type and that possess properties that no longer have anything in common with the starting point; or better, it achieves results that explain the starting point in a way that no longer has anything material about it. And if our science can do this, ought not we to conclude that there is within us a power that transcends matter, that reaches beyond the empirical sense knowledge that comes from matter and remains on the same level as matter?

3. Result of Explanation

What is the end product of the scientific process? Let us take it first of all on the level of a simple explanation in its most spontaneous form—the case of the man who reasons only seldom or little. It will be worth our while to stop here a moment because the result is enlightening.

When the average man comes face to face with a new object or fact, how does he explain it? Psychologists have detected several stages in his thought process which are often telescoped together in actual reality: he relates the new fact to other facts that he knows from other sources and that he recalls from memory, he develops new insights, eliminates aspects that he considers secondary, etc.

But what is the main result? It is *the elaboration of an idea* expressed in a concept. I form an idea of a certain object that I am going to buy, I form an idea of such and such a person who interests me. What does that mean? Very simply, in a series of mental comparisons and eliminations, I am seeking to create in my mind a representation of the object or the person that is as exact as possible. But note that there is no question here of forming a mental picture from sheer memory, an image made up of primitive sense data. I can keep in my memory the image of such and such a person who is not now present before me; by means of this image I can visualize him with all his living richness, his physical appearance, voice, bearing, etc. But this is not yet an idea of him, a tentative explanation of what he really is. In recalling his likeness to mind, I have progressed no further than when I actually saw him.

In fact, an image remains at the material level; it is the result of a sensation, the material modification of an organ, and it provides nothing more than that. On the contrary, an idea is begotten at a higher, more refined, more abstract level. It is the result of a rational analysis and allows me to say about the person whom I recall that he is of such and such a kind, such and such a quality, etc. If I combine and regroup some characteristics which in themselves are only general, then, by attributing them to the person who is materially represented by the image, I shall arrive at a fairly accurate idea of him, that is, a rational type of representation that will be a true enrichment for me, a new knowledge. None of the elements of this idea are truly new, but my combining and attributing them to a concrete subject is new. The idea that I then form of that person will explain his conduct to me; in a word, I shall know what he is.

Hence ideas are the great means whereby material objects can be explained and understood; they are like indicators pointing out the structure of reality; and obviously they vary with the depth in which reality is studied. On the macroscopic level, the level of daily life and classical science, ideas can very well be clear and simple to conceive. Thus they can express the qualities of a human being (e.g., X is an idiot, or he is well-educated, or has an undershot jaw) equally as well as those of a chemical substance (CH_4 is colorless, tasteless and odorless)—all qualities that are in reference to daily experience and the memory of a sensation.

But at the atomic as well as at the astronomical level, modern science is obliged to express the intelligibility it seeks in language to which sensory terms of reference contribute nothing at all. Indeed, modern science can no longer express what it knows about reality by using macroscopic data, the only ones it normally had at its disposal (the universe of Euclid or Galileo) until now. Science is obliged to hammer out new and very different mathematical concepts, which say nothing to the imagination and which are far removed from all reference to human experience or even ordinary common sense (e.g., non-Euclidean geometries, four-dimensional space, the complimentarity of wave-corpuscles, the triumph of the axiomatic, etc.). From the very beginning all attempts to use diagrams or plans based on macroscopic data proved futile. On this point, the history of the various models of the atom made since Rutherford's (1911) tells us a lot about this scientific revolution which has resulted in replacing figurative representations by others that are purely operative (the theory of groups).[3]

Hence the kind of intelligibility or explanation that modern science aims at is quite different from that sought by classical science or common sense, for it tends more and more toward a veritable dematerialization of mental symbols, toward almost absolute independence from sense data. Nevertheless, this is not a real break or discontinuity but rather an advance, because even at the child's level any explanatory idea reveals a certain independence from concrete matter, an independence that becomes total in modern science.

4. Ideas Embodied in Matter

Although ideas are formed by human thought exercising its rational powers, they are not pure creations but have been formed or

[3] Regarding this evolution, see H. L. Searles, *Logic and Scientific Methods* (New York, The Ronald Press Company, 1948); H. Reichenbach, *The Rise of Scientific Philosophy* (Berkeley, University of California Press, 1951); *International Encyclopedia of Unified Science*, O. Neurath, P. Carnap, and C. Morris, eds. (2 vols., Chicago, University of Chicago Press, 1955); C. Singer and others, *A History of Technology* (5 vols., New York, Oxford University Press, 1958).

extracted from objective data. These data, however, are on a different level, the level of sensation and imagination. This forming or elaboration of ideas involves what we call an abstraction (in the active and operative meaning of the term). Thus to abstract means to disregard a certain number of secondary, non-essential characteristics provided by sensation and imagination in order to throw into relief a universal, intelligible value. Therefore an abstraction is not a mutilation or a destruction of reality but is, on the contrary, the *normal process for apprehending the truth of reality* in all its fullness. For example, I know what my father meant to me, what distinguished him from all other men; but I was able to evolve my personal concept of him only by leaving aside the myriad details of sense data that I had collected about him, data which, moreover, had continually changed as he grew older, such as his physique, color of hair, and timbre of voice. Obviously, if I did not remember these sense data to which I can refer my concept, the knowledge of my father that I have derived by abstraction would be dry and lifeless. This would also be true in the case of persons who had not known my father personally and who therefore knew nothing about him except what I or someone else told them.

Thus, an idea appears as embodied in and demanding contact with reality by the reason of its very origin and the process of abstraction that begets it. But conversely, we take an idea that we have created ourselves by sheer thought and embody it in a material form by means of an image (creative imagination), a visible plan, or a model. Thus an idea's independence of the world of matter is revealed here as plainly as in the inverse process (extraction of the idea) because the same idea can be actualized in different ways, in various materials. So an engineer's skill is shown in his ability to embody or put into effect a project, a single idea, in many forms (depending upon the materials at his disposal) and in a theoretically unlimited number of copies.

For example, a mysterious instrument, found on board a reconnaissance plane belonging to a foreign power, has been handed to a military expert for examination. It is the expert's job to find out the enemy's reason for making the instrument. This means more than merely ascertaining what the instrument is used for, although the layman generally stops at this stage and hence his ideas are merely superficial. The expert goes further. Even if he finds out what the instrument is (e.g., a simple radio direction-finder), he will want to delve deeper to discover how it achieves its general purpose. Then he can judge whether or not that purpose could have been attained in another way, more simply, or whether, on the contrary, it has been reached in an unexpected manner. The purpose for which the apparatus was devised is then apparent in two forms: as embodied in the actual instrument (by a special arrangement of pieces of metal of certain definite shapes), and also as independent of this particular type of instrument, because it can be achieved in some other way.

Suppose further that the military expert has his dog with him while he is working. The animal sees everything his master sees and can possess as exact a sense knowledge of the instrument as he; indeed, the dog can sense some data more sharply than its master, owing, for example, to its keener sense of smell. But that will be all. The animal will stop there, confined to the material, sense level, the only world in which its life unfolds. The expert, on the contrary, using the same sense data, but also by evoking memories and images of similar instruments, by establishing abstract relationships between the disassembled pieces, will build up in his mind an idea of the instrument that will allow him to know exactly what it is. Then we can say that the immaterial idea which the maker embodied in a particular way in the instrument has been rediscovered by the expert. And where was that idea? It was present everywhere, fully and completely, both in each part that had been shaped and assembled to achieve the purpose of the instrument and also in the instrument as a whole. That obviously means that the idea behind the instrument transcends the material, which is one specific substance (steel or Duralumin, but not both at once) and which is in this one spot and not elsewhere. The idea, on the other hand, by a kind of mysterious existence, is found everywhere under different appearances: in the mind of the builder, in that of the expert, in the details of the instrument and in the whole apparatus itself. Hence we can see that the idea behind the instrument has a strange independence, a basic polyvalence; the idea cries aloud its immateriality through the curtain of its embodiment in matter.

This world from which the embodied idea draws its nature and properties shows, through ideas, that it is as real as the world of matter. It has been given a name, the world of spirit. The term "spirit" therefore has not been invented to meet the needs of a cause, to cover up a religious illusion, to designate an act of faith. No, it is a *reality* that reveals itself to us in the normal exercise of even the smallest intellectual activity, in the elaboration of the most commonplace idea as well as in that of the most sublime concept. It is also found elsewhere, in more exalted circumstances, as we shall see in the chapters that follow. But even at this stage we can draw the logical conclusion, that if ideas are of such a nature, then human thought, whose product they are, must be even more emphatically of the same type; it must belong to a world that is not the world of matter. There must exist in man an inner spiritual (i.e., non-material) center of activity; hence we can suspect that this center of activity will radiate the same spiritual power in other areas of human life as it does in knowing the material world. Even in the very commonplace process of forming ideas, man shows that he possesses a power that distinguishes him from the animal and demonstrates that he belongs to the spiritual world. How much more, then, must this ability shine forth in the whole complex of human life?

II. SPIRIT PRESENT IN MATTER

Having reached this conclusion, we can now better discern the relationship between the two realities that we call matter and spirit. They appear to be completely different from each other in their essential natures and yet they overlap strangely.

1. Difference between Matter and Spirit

An analysis of the properties of the two worlds of matter and spirit indicates at first a fundamental opposition in their methods, an irreconcilable difference that shows itself as we approach the mystery of the spiritual.

(a) The World of Matter, Domain of Quantity

Matter is everything that is seen, felt or touched, that is measurable and localized, that is detected by some change or other which is generally marked by a space-time modification. In more exact terms, matter is characterized by *extension, divisibility,* by the property of perceptibly separate or separable parts (cf. the debate about the continuous and the discontinuous).

Matter is the direct object of both common and scientific human knowledge. Even at its most spiritual, scientific knowledge begins with sense knowledge, the contact of the human body with its surroundings (first by an organic change in a sensory receptor, and then essentially by this change's being assimilated by the brain, which integrates sensations). In this way the world of matter reaches man, who is plunged into it by his own body; and so, at the human level, the term "material" is synonymous with "organic."

(b) The World of Spirit and Reflective Thought

By the very nature of its origin, our method of knowing does not open directly upon the world of the spirit. We are able to become aware of this other world only by means of a kind of deduction, in contrast to the way in which we know about matter. Thus we judge the spiritual, too, in terms of that which is *not* seen or touched, that which does *not* lend itself to being grasped and measured by the senses. The spiritual is that which *in itself* cannot be localized (although it is localized in the sense of being embodied in something material). Above all, the spiritual cannot be subject to extension and hence it is not subject to division or dismemberment.

The philosopher will say that the attribute of the spiritual that sums up its rejection of the characteristics of matter is *simplicity,* as opposed to something made up of separate or separable parts. By its *simplicity,* the spiritual in its pure state is, in its own order, situated outside space and time.

There is certainly a less material method of approaching the spiritual but we deliberately did not choose it because our purpose was precisely to discover the world of the spirit by starting from its most familiar form, its embodiment in matter. The other method, though it gives a more clear-cut result, does presuppose self-reflection, and we merely mention it here to remark that it is the method of "self-consciousness," awareness of self in the very act of knowing.

For example, I am conscious that I find it hard to read a very small variation of electrical current on the dial of an ammeter. Consequently, I doubt the accuracy of my reading, I am conscious of my doubt, and I refrain from drawing any conclusion from my reading. This means that, in the act of reflecting on my own knowledge, I am at once the object (myself as I doubt my reading) and the subject (I am aware that I'm doubtful). Now, this doubling back on self, this possibility of self-reflection, of standing back from the very act of knowing, of looking at oneself while acting or experiencing, is incompatible with a knowledge that is strictly organic and material. Such self-reflection implies a disinterestedness of action, a detachment in looking squarely at one's own actions, and it is clear evidence that reflection is a perfect type of abstraction, of freedom from the tangible, the material.

(c) Man on the Border between the Two Worlds

Therefore, the scope of our knowledge embraces realities of *two contradictory or opposite types,* those of the two worlds of matter and spirit. Between these two worlds there is a real break, a radical *discontinuity,* whence comes the impossibility of passing gradually from one to the other. In their case, the law of all or nothing prevails because the characteristics by which they reveal themselves cannot be gathered together within a more general category of which they would be merely two different forms. This is so because the characteristics of the spirit are the negation of those of matter.[4]

But man is in a privileged situation; his is a truly dramatic life, because he is part of both these worlds. The dividing line between

---

[4] That is the reason why we can say that human thought, insofar as it is spiritual, cannot be the product of the brain, which is a purely material organ. That is also why, in the context of evolution, the human soul cannot have resulted from a development of animal psychological activity. Hence the paleontologist will say with Teilhard de Chardin that between man and everything that preceded him there is a change of state, a clean break. See *The Phenomenon of Man* (New York, Harper & Row Publishers, 1961) p. 303.

matter and spirit passes through him; he is a living hinge joining the two, and as such he is subject to many conflicting restraints and attractions.

If we examine this dualism with a naive conception of what the spiritual is, we may conclude not only that our lives must be a continual struggle between matter and spirit, but also that we must devote all our energies to seeking a balance that is impossible from the outset because such contradictory elements can never be reconciled.

This dilemma arises when we concentrate too much on the differences between the two worlds of matter and spirit. In every age these differences have greatly tempted men to adopt a kind of Manichaeism, for there has always been a strong urge to envisage a dynamic opposition between matter, as the source of all evil, and spirit, as the principle of all that is good.

But strangely enough, despite their irreconcilable differences, it is impossible to think of the two worlds as being in real opposition to each other. They are not just two of a kind, since they do not partake of reality in precisely similar degrees. Since we are able to reach the spiritual by starting from the material, it is evident that matter is deeply impregnated with spirit. This aspect of the problem is really a complement of the first aspect, the dissimilarity between the world of spirit and the world of matter. Let us now examine this essential point, the source of union between the two worlds.

2. Spirit in Matter

The mere fact that knowledge of matter has made it possible for us to discover spirit is a lesson in itself: namely, that although spirit is different from matter, spirit nevertheless plays a dynamic role in regard to matter by being present in it and penetrating it deeply.

But it is easy to become confused when we hear people talking about the presence of spirit in matter, as we shall see in the next chapter. This confusion consists in thinking that spirit can be present in matter in only one form, whereas a brief examination of the facts shows that we must distinguish two essentially different forms of the presence of spirit in matter.

(a) First Form: Matter Bears the Marks of Spirit

Here we are dealing essentially with a penetration, *a passive participation,* proved by the simple fact that every corporeal or material thing has a definite structure, a particular nature which it manifests by properties that are special to it and which permit it to be classified. This holds true at any level of existence, from the galaxy to the atom. St. Thomas calls this special attribute a "form," that is, *a mode of organization,* the face which each corporeal being presents to the world, making it intelligible.

A comparison with human workmanship is enlightening here. Man can take a material element that is already determined in its own order (wood or metal) and give it a new structure, a special shape, for a precise aim (by carving a statue or building a motor). That is to say, he can embody in a given material an idea conceived by his creative thought. Naturally, the actual execution of his idea will be influenced by the material he uses, by matter. In similar fashion, even in its natural state matter contains within it structures or organizations that can be disclosed by man's efforts. Thus matter already carries within it the vestiges of spirit.

In fact, the idea by which man expresses what he understands about matter is not the pure creation of his reason. Instead, this idea must have some foundation in the object studied and must be present to man, not in the same way that it is ordinarily present in his mind (as an abstract universal concept), but rather in a concrete, matter-related way.

In other words, matter is passively impregnated with a mode of spiritual presence, in much the same fashion as a product of human skill is impregnated with the thought of its builder. *Otherwise, matter would be unintelligible,* and we, whether scientists or laymen, could say nothing about it. We shall see in chapter four the logical conclusion to be drawn from the traces which spirit has left in matter.

(b) Second Form: Spirit Actively Present through Human Thought

On the other hand, in the midst of this material world another form of spirit, human thought, reveals its presence in a very special, *dynamic* way. In fact, man is not simply a passive organization, structure or nature, like material beings in general. He is, at the same time, an active spiritual being. He discovers in nature the traces or imprints of spirit like impressions on wax, and thus he collects knowledge either popular or scientific. Or he can act upon matter in order to give it a new structure, thus engaging in art and technology. Whichever he does, he gives meaning to matter, discovering that it is intelligible or giving it a new intelligibility. Hence, by his thought man begets a dynamic form of spirit embodied in matter.

The essential thing, then, is to understand that there is a deep abyss between this presence of spirit "infused" into matter by man's mind and the simple traces of spirit in matter that we mentioned before. In the latter, spirit shows itself only by its vestiges, its participation; it is not really present in matter on the same level as the matter itself, which retains its autonomy and unbroken consistency. But in the former case we find spirit itself, in the form of human participation, acting with all its power in the heart of the material world through the medium of the human body.[5]

3. Materialism versus Spiritualism [5a]

It would be a grave mistake to forget the difference between these two ways in which spirit can impregnate matter. The whole ideological conflict between materialists and the defenders of the spiritual is often aggravated by this error.

(a) The Temptation to Anthropomorphism

Indeed, the history of thought shows that men have always been tempted to explain the various mysteries of nature by presupposing that each is caused by a particular spirit, regarded as being like the human soul, a demiurge or an angel, a sort of *deus ex machina*. Although intelligibility is preserved by this facile, childish explana-

[5] The philosopher would say that the first form of spirit's presence in matter ("infused" by man's mind) is an example of *formal* participation, while the second is *material* participation.

[5a] We use this word here in its primary meaning, "the view that spirit is a prime element of reality": *Webster's Seventh New Collegiate Dictionary* (1963). (*Translator's Note*)

tion, those who proposed it forgot that the spirit at work in non-human nature cannot be compared with man's soul and its activities. (In chapter four we shall speak about what has been called the transcendent, analogical nature of this universal spiritual activity.) However, because of confused thinking, it was believed that nature bears traces of the spiritual, of an organized plan (material participation), and so there was an inclination to imagine, without any proof, that each material thing had a special spiritual principle that explained its activity and structure, especially if it seemed mysterious, the whole concept being a sort of extension of the human spiritual principle.

As we shall see in the next chapter, this type of animism or *generalized vitalism* is a gross caricature of an analogical divine action that transcends that of creatures. It still survives among many contemporary writers who appeal to a mysterious, more or less spiritual, vital principle to explain the mystery of life on the simple level of plants and animals. This is merely an extension, under another form, of the medieval theory that there are angels who have the special duty of moving the crystal spheres supporting the stars.

Such naive spiritualism, often accompanied by confused notions of anthropomorphism, has its counterpart in an equally-naive materialism that frequently disregards the most elementary shades of meaning.

(b) What Is Materialism?

The term materialism is a classical example of a word so vague and inexact that it can mean many different things, some acceptable, others not. Much of the regrettable misunderstanding so frequent in the history of the conflict between science and faith comes from this inexactness.

The only meaning of the word "materialism" that is unacceptable to Christians as well as to anyone who sincerely wishes to understand reality as a whole is materialism taken to signify a denial of the world of the spirit, a denial of God or the human soul. In this sense of the term, matter is the only reality, the only thing that really exists. When materialism is understood in this way, it is a *metaphysical* concept. Because it admits the existence of only one reality, matter, it is one form of monism (from the Greek word *monos*, meaning "alone" or "only"), the other form being idealism, which holds that thought is the only reality.[6]

Insofar as it is a rejection of the world of the spirit, this metaphysical materialism is in contradiction to what our search for the spirit has shown us. Besides denying the existence of God, it refuses to see in man the presence of an active spiritual principle. And since its proponents can scarcely refuse to admit that matter is intelligible—(to do otherwise would be absurd) it is hard to see how they can refuse to admit that man has a power capable of reaching that intelligibility.

As we have seen, *the existence of spirit is not a mere assumption*, a preconceived notion. By that we simply mean to say that in man there exists a faculty that allows him to cope with matter, to make himself independent of it so as to better understand it. If we rightly understand the intelligibility of matter and the ability of scientific knowledge to penetrate it, we are led inevitably to the conclusion that thought itself cannot be material. This is so because each type of material thing has a different structure and its own special nature, with the result that different material types cannot communicate with each other in a unifying act such as rational knowledge.

Because man's spirit is not limited to a particular structure, as is each thing in nature, it is always ready and capable of freeing itself from knowledge that it already possesses in order to accept new knowledge. That is what we mean when we say that human thought is non-material, or spiritual; and that is only simple logic.

Therefore, materialism, taken in the metaphysical sense of rejecting the world of the spirit, is an irrational solution. Its proponents are often motivated by sentiment or emotion, which is as much a determining factor in their case as it is with some of the more short-sighted defenders of man's spiritual nature.

[6] The principal forms of materialism are *positivism* and *epiphenomenism*. *Positivism* is concerned only with tangible, material data—an illogical position because all scientific endeavor is aimed precisely at going beyond these data. *Epiphenomenism* regards thought as being merely a transitory, useless by-product of the completely material activity of the brain; although the two phenomena, neural and spiritual, may influence each other, their characteristics are too diverse to admit of a common origin.

(b) Scientific Materialism

On the other hand, the whole complexion of the problem changes if by materialism we mean simply the doctrine that tries to explain bodily, material beings *on the level of scientific explanation* and without appealing to a spiritual principle. In fact, apart from the angels, whose existence is known only through faith, there are, in the whole universe, only two active spirits, one of which is dependent on the other: God, whose transcendent action eludes scientific observation (while still being discernible by reasoned thought), and the human soul at work in the world. Hence, when we seek a scientific explanation of the material world, it is not only normal to avoid appealing to any special spiritual principle, it is in fact the only logically acceptable attitude.

Let us be clear on this. We are here concerned only with an explanation of material beings (living or inorganic) that remains at the level of scientific facts, things that can be measured and localized. This attitude is perfectly compatible with the one that begins with the traces of spirit in matter and tries to deduce from this the existence of a Spirit, the source of all intelligibility. There we are not on the scientific level but on the level of common sense or of metaphysics. Hence, there can be no opposition between the two approaches.

There is only one domain in which this so-called scientific materialism will have to be less rigid—in the sciences dealing with man. Spirit is present in man's body as it is in all material things (in the sense we have explained above), but that is by no means all. Man also possesses a truly *active* spiritual principle. Again, denying the existence of this principle, the soul, would be to mutilate reality at the human level. We shall say more about this point in the next chapter when we are dealing with the implications of materialism in biology.

Materialism, such as that of the physicist, chemist and biologist, is the only possible method of approach and the only logical philosophy at the level of scientific research. In man alone does there exist a created spiritual principle which demands to be taken into special consideration. His animal nature cannot be absolutely isolated from the whole of his being, impregnated as it is with the soul, the human spiritual principle. In addition, where man is concerned, scientific materialism cannot claim to be the only true scientific attitude because account must be taken of the demands of spirituality. Even when scientific materialism is regarded solely as a method (leaving aside all consideration of the spiritual, without prejudice), it presents some disadvantages which theologians such as Dubarle have rightly stressed, because *a method always presupposes a doctrine.*

(d) Marxist Materialism

Marxist materialism has continually tried to present itself as scientific materialism, as opposed to the "bourgeois" materialism of the last century. But when we examine the matter more closely we see at once that when the Marxists speak about *scientific* materialism they mean precisely what we have just described as metaphysical materialism, the absolute denial of every form of spirit, whether God or the human soul, for reasons that have nothing scientific about them but are really only assumptions.

As we shall see, the problem of God's existence does not arise from scientific observation, and to deny that he exists is not a scientific position, but rather a philosophical one. The existence and spirituality of the human soul are demonstrated by reasoned thought, as we saw above, and to deny it would be to deny all validity to the smallest reflective examination of the process of knowing.[7]

Marxist materialism therefore has adopted the metaphysical materialism described above as its doctrinal basis. In this regard, then, Marxist teaching presents nothing new. But it is interesting to note that Marxism has not stopped there. With remarkable intuition and shrewd reasoning its founders took this metaphysical materialism, which they often coated with sugar before presenting it for consumption, and grafted on to it additional theses that have the merit of emphasizing truths that are too often forgotten. This explains the dangerous appeal of their so-called dialectical and historical materialism.

[7] On Marxism, see M. D'Arcy, S.J., *Communism and Christianity* (Baltimore, Penguin Books, Inc., 1956); C. Dawson, *Religion and the Modern State* (New York, Sheed & Ward, 1938); F. J. Sheen, *Communism and the Conscience of the West* (Indianapolis, The Bobbs-Merrill Company, Inc., 1948).

What are these new theses? First of all, matter is no longer regarded as something inert, as it was in the mechanistic outlook of classical materialism. Rather it is conceived as being essentially *dynamic,* for reasons of simple logic. The moment all presence of spirit was denied in matter, the old materialism could not explain the forces at work in it; it was therefore necessary to regard matter as being dynamic. That is all very well, but the whole point is: Does this make the denial of the existence of spirit any more logical? When we speak of forces and dynamism, we must imply orientation; we have in mind a purposeful structure in a well-defined sense. We can therefore ask ourselves if Marxism, in its criticism of spirit, has not begun from a caricature of it, conceiving it as being static or as a reality that comes from outside of animate matter. On this point, let us not forget that the adversaries who fought Marx and Engels were proponents of idealism or completely disembodied spiritualism, with whom the adherents of traditional Christian spirituality (especially those such as St. Thomas) had very little in common. We think, too, that the Marxist criticisms are plainly seen to be wrong and unacceptable when they are examined in relation to a more responsible and realistic idea of the spiritual than the one they often present to the world.

Morever, Marxism insists on the dependence of beings upon each other, on the general movement that animates them all as they progress in a dialectical movement (by contradiction). These are some ideas and insights that can, and even must, be included in a spiritualist synthesis of reality that wishes to take into account the most coherent vision of the world revealed by modern science. The whole Thomistic concept of nature is based on the fact of change, which St. Thomas explained by the doctrine of Aristotelian hylomorphism (matter and form). It would therefore be doubly regrettable to allow Marxism to claim unchallenged the benefits of this intuition. It is curious that some Marxists, such as Garaudy, do not hesitate to annex the thought of a man like Teilhard de Chardin, who was so concerned about this aspect of reality. However, this attempt at annexation, far from bothering us and making us suspect the author of *The Phenomenon of Man,* should instead urge us on to pursue his line of thought. In our final chapter we shall see Teilhard's profound and genuine spiritualism, and we shall deal with the problem in more detail.

Marxism also insists upon the importance of economic facts, to the point of seeing in them the basic explanation of man's evolution. Here too a completely disembodied spirituality has been an easy target. We shall see in chapter five, when we speak about the theology of work, that Christians have no cause to envy the Marxists in a true assessment of this truth. The exaggerated importance which Marxist philosophers give the economic factor springs from their denial that man has a transcendent spiritual destiny. We shall deal with this point in chapter four.

Finally, in chapter five we shall examine, in the light of Christ's role in human history, Marxism's last characteristic, its emphasis on *the meaning of history*. Too many Christians have forgotten that, in following Christ and his Church, they are irrevocably committed to an essentially historical inheritance. Here again Marxism has exploited a truth to which modern man is very sensitive. Our task will be to show how history and its implications can be integrated into the Christian synthesis.

When confronted with the different forms of true materialism (metaphysical and Marxist), we are forced to the conclusion that too often they have been embraced so readily only because they met with no opposition except a childish, *disembodied spiritualism* that often abandoned to materialism truths which it should have integrated into its own system and which, although they were traditional, it was unable to recognize under the new appearances they had assumed. One of the principal reasons for this shortsightedness was the exaggeration of *Cartesian dualism* which, having divorced spirit from matter, then left matter outside the orbit and influence of the spirit. Add to that a *pessimistic tendency*—the old temptation to Manichaeism—to belittle matter or to see in it a principle that, while it might not be evil, was at least foreign to any truly human life. Thus, the field was left free for exploitation by the materialism that came in the wake of the rapid progress scientists made from their starting point, the material universe.

4. Conclusion

At the end of this twofold investigation, reaching spiritual values by analyzing the workings of human reason and by examining the reciprocal relationships between spirit and matter, we are able to see better the benefit that can come from a more coherent and balanced view of reality as a whole, namely, a greater ease in uniting concretely these two worlds that meet in man.

To continue this effort, we shall deal more thoroughly in the next chapter with the *biological and human* aspects of the problem, examining it on the level not only of knowledge but also of freedom and love.

Hence, we can already say that the spirit that we have found by our investigation cannot be a mere reflection of matter but is, on the contrary, that which gives matter its value. Just as the sun gives us light to see the outer appearance of things, so too does the spirit make the world luminous and intelligible to our inner eye. But in spite of this, spirit cannot be confused with things outside it, for its function is to penetrate all of them by its light. It must remain independent of them, while still being ready to understand them; it must remain unyieldingly itself, yet always be prepared to welcome them. To play this role is what Paul Valéry calls "the undefined refusal to be any one particular thing, no matter what that thing may be."

III

LIFE AND FREEDOM

We have seen that a great dividing line cuts across the world, splitting it into two domains, one of matter, the other of spirit. These profoundly interact upon each other despite the great difference between them, the world of matter deriving its very value and intelligibility from the impregnation of spirit. "Matter is not a separate substance, a creature in its own right, but is rather both a connecting link and at the same time a divider. It performs an essential function in the overall plan of the universe, including even the spiritual element." [1]

Yet, through this basic hierarchy another fact becomes evident, at the very heart of these two worlds, manifesting a progressive shading of one into the other. It is the major phenomenon of the living world, immersed on the one hand in matter (plants and animals) and culminating on the other hand in the realm of the spirit (man).

How are we to situate this phenomenon in relation to the cosmic division that concerns us here? That is what we must inquire into now, looking at the matter first in general and then going on to determine the superior, spiritual form that life assumes in man.

[1] M. Blondel, *La Pensée,* Vol. I (Paris, Presses Universitaires de France), p. 278.

I. LIFE

1. False Statements of the Problem

The question of the nature and origin of life has been so long a favorite battlefield for the conflict between science and faith that even today the state of the problem is often falsified by an unspoken *preoccupation with apologetics,* the remainders of the struggles of the last century, so much so that we must start with a clarification. From this very fact we shall be able more easily to make a presentation of the phenomenon of life more in conformity with classical Christian teaching because it will be stripped of useless prejudices.

(a) The Collusion between Vitalists and Spiritualists

Indeed, from the very moment we begin to tackle the problem, especially from a historical point of view, we find ourselves faced with a rather frightening fact. Since the conflict between science and religion of the last century, this problem has been posed in such a fashion that a number of Catholic scientists, generally ignorant of theology, have been led into a position which, far from being demanded by the Faith, is actually opposed to the teaching of classical Catholic thought. The result has been a lamentable misunderstanding on the part of scientists who are less concerned with religious matters. They were led astray by what was falsely presented to them as being bound up with the Christian concept of life.

The modern theologian who has most clearly stated his condemnation of this mistake, in the name of the thought of St. Thomas and of classical theology, did not hesitate to write: "Current explanations of life are divided into two clearly defined categories. The first school of thought, usually called the materialistic school, regards living things as material bodies that are distinguished from inanimate objects only by their basic structure. That is the solution that we shall support. . . . The second school, generally called the vitalist school, believes that life can be explained only by the intervention of a spirit whose role is further-more regarded in very different ways by various authors." [2]

Whence comes the misunderstanding? Classical theology divided the universe, as we have seen in the preceding chapter, into the realm of the spirit (God, angels or pure spirits, and the human soul) and that of matter (all dimensional substances, from the simplest chemical element, through all living things, up to the human body). Only for man, sharing as he does in both realms, is the capital problem of unity posed.

In modern times (since the seventeenth century), particularly in the nineteenth century and even in our day (for instance in Berg-son) the so-called "spiritualist" concept is used in a very different way: "Instead of contrasting matter with spirit, as before, they now contrast it with living things. The created world is once more split into two radically opposite domains, but the frontier has been shifted. Henceforth living things will form a fundamental category, which includes man and therefore all his prestige as a spiritual, self-knowing, intelligent, and self-directed being. Because this category also includes animals, plants, and protozoa, it reflects upon them some of man's transcendent values. This category contains a homogeneous series of things which must be defended as a whole, and henceforth the most essential religious and moral principles will appear as dependent upon the concept one has of the most modest living thing. What is most striking about this new doctrine is that it is substituted for the old one so imperceptibly that a number of authors have adopted it without realizing the originality of their position. Nothing is more curious, in this respect, than the philosophers who call themselves Thomists, who want to be and sincerely think they are such, but who think that on that account they must contrast matter with life, thus following a plan that is radically foreign to the thought of their supposed teacher, St. Thomas. A basic source of contemporary vitalism springs from a reading of Aristotle and St. Thomas, interpreted in the light of the strange dichotomy whose dubious origins we have exposed." [3]

---

[2] D. H. Salman, "La bio-philosophie récente" in *Revue des Sciences philosophiques et théologiques,* (October, 1949), pp. 390-426. At present, many theologians who are interested in the question share this opinion (e.g., Moretti, S.J., and Bauchau, S.J., cited in footnote 4 below).

[3] Salman, *op. cit.,* p. 393.

What is the origin of this lamentable mistake, which still weighs heavily upon the scientific world in the idea it has formed of the demands of the faith? It is apologetic in nature and is rooted in an anthropomorphic concept of God and his action in the world. We shall examine it in more detail in the next chapter. Here we shall quickly summarize this childish concept of God's action, which is imagined as a series of many operations, somewhat like those of a craftsman making one piece of furniture after another. Thus God is put on the same plane as his creatures, just as in bygone ages people thought that he acted directly on the stars whose mysterious movements were a proof of his existence. Then, when Newton found the reason for the regularity of this movement, another "mystery" had to be discovered in which God's action could take refuge, as it were; the answer was found in life, whose complexity seemed to defy for all time an exhaustive scientific explanation. And the better to insure this mysterious refuge, each living thing was supposed to contain a certain unexplainable something that would elude the grasp of science, the famous *vital principle,* which was the expression of God's action on it. Special interventions by God were multiplied at will, but the proponents of the theory forgot that theology has always placed God's transcendent and immanent action at the heart of created causality, which it does not at all eliminate. We shall see, further on, that basically this concept is insulting to God, denying the proper nature, and consequently the dignity, of his action in the world.

(b) Confusing Scientific with Metaphysical Materialism

The results of this error were grave. Biologists who were rightly convinced that, apart from the human soul, life is only a special organization of matter, were often regarded *en bloc* as being among the enemies of religion and were treated as vulgar materialists. This opprobrious title, when applied to them, confused the unacceptable doctrine of metaphysical materialism (denial of the spiritual in all forms, whether as God or as the human soul) and scientific materialism (refusal to appeal to a vital principle, foreign to matter, in every living thing), a doctrine which is in harmony with Christian tradition. The two theories were completely mixed together, although they have nothing to do with each other; scientific materialism can, without any contradiction, be integrated into genuine spiritualism. But the vitalist literature, which is still being produced, proclaimed aloud that the techniques of modern so-called "materialistic" biology (trying to explain life in terms of the characteristics of matter) were in contradiction to the Faith. As a result the mere fact of stating the contrary proposition evoked surprise and even scandalized some people. The solution of the conflict between materialism and spiritualism therefore must not be sought on the level of biology; instead, it ought to enter a more general area, as we tried to sketch at the end of the preceding chapter.

(c) Will Science Succeed in Producing Life?

Another consequence of the confusion is the idea, which many believers have fixed in their minds, that science will never be able to produce life, precisely because life shares completely in the dignity of the spirit whose independence from matter obviously demands a divine intervention at its origin. In fact, this is true only in the case of the human soul. When we have discussed the real theological meaning of creation in the next chapter, we shall see more clearly that, from the religious point of view, this is a false problem.

But even now we can easily understand that if a living thing is composed only of material elements without any strange and contradictory spiritual principle, its creation by science would be merely a transformation of pre-existing materials; only the structure or organization would be different. If scientists produce life from inanimate elements they will have gone from the relative simplicity of inorganic matter to the extraordinary complexity of living things. That is the only problem, and it is a strictly scientific one—precise knowledge of the laws of biology.

The majority of biologists now believe that such a feat is not only possible but feasible. Look at the hopes raised by Stanley Miller's experiments in reconstructing a living organism from simple elements, that is, endeavoring to reconstitute the physico-chemical conditions favorable to life that existed when life originated on our planet. And consider also Fraenkel-Conrat's experiments—

recombining once living but now inert elements with a view to obtaining a true virus.[4]

These possibilities should not distress the Christian but should rather encourage him for he has nothing against the hypothesis that biochemistry will one day succeed in producing life in the laboratory in a form even more complex than a simple protozoön. From a philosophical and religious point of view, synthesizing a living thing is the same type of procedure as synthesizing any organic compound, although it is, to be sure, infinitely more elaborate. Only our ignorance of how physico-chemical laws work at the very special level of living things prevents us from producing life in the laboratory.

(d) Saint Thomas Believed in Spontaneous Generation

Here we are again faced with one of the consequences of this misunderstanding. Nowadays we know that spontaneous generation, that is, the appearance of life apart from a germ of some kind, is impossible. But we are convinced of this for *scientific reasons* and not for religious or philosophical ones.

To the vitalist, spontaneous generation seemed like a denial of that mysterious divine intervention which was presupposed at the origin of each species and which the vital principle should prolong by being passed on from generation to generation. But if this is so, why not presuppose the same intervention at the origin of each chemical compound? And we must admit that the interest which Pasteur's famed experiments aroused in spiritualist circles was mainly apologetic (and very shortsighted).

What, then, would those who despise spontaneous generation have said if they had read St. Thomas's words upholding it? Following Aristotle, the great theologian did in fact believe that certain inferior living things were begotten by putrefaction merely as the result of physical causes (the heat of the sun), exactly the contrary of what our modern vitalists held.[5] Indeed, this idea was

[4] On these experiments and their religious or philosophical repercussions, see Bauchau, "Vers une synthèse artificielle de la Vie" in *Nouvelle Revue théologique* (1958), pp. 395ff.; and Moretti, "Les virus et la synthèse de la Vie" in *Etudes* (1956), pp. 81ff.

[5] Aristotle, *On the Generation of Animals*, III. 11; St. Thomas, *Summa Theologica*, I, q. 71, a. 1, ad 1.

generally accepted until the eighteenth century when the question began to be freely debated between two churchmen, Spallanzani and Needham. And if we today do not believe in spontaneous generation it is solely because there is no longer any trace of the balanced physical conditions that existed at the beginning of the geological ages and that permitted the emergence of life, conditions which patient researchers dream of reproducing in the laboratory in order to solve the problem of synthesizing life (always provided, of course, that the time factor, so important in geology, is not indispensable).

(e) Finality or Determinism?

It would be impossible to name all the consequences of the vitalist confusion that has contributed to falsifying many bio-philosophical problems. The case of the abuse of finality in biology is an important result, because to be a supporter of finality in biology has been for a long time, and still is to some extent, the same as being a spiritualist. Here too the metaphysical and scientific planes have been confused.

From the metaphysical point of view, the principle of finality has absolutely nothing in it that a scientist would find objectionable because it is only *the logical expression of determinism,* precisely the opposite of what the scientific materialists (who reject it) and the vitalists (who defend it) think it is.

In fact, finality, the subject of debate in biology, is viewed as if it were human finality, conscious finality. This is the result of a kind of unacceptable transfer inspired by the same confusion between the two types of living things, material and spiritual. Thus the vitalists make this kind of finality a principle of every living thing, as if each such thing had the property of being able to organize itself and direct itself toward a mysterious end, by an instinct which they are unwilling to explain and apart from any explanation from the point of view of physico-chemical causality. Hence it is clear that the opponents of vitalism have had great fun in ridiculing this application of human finality to a field that has nothing at all to do with it.

But what is finality, anyway? The old maxim explains it briefly: "Every agent acts for an end." That is, everything that acts, that changes or evolves, necessarily tends toward an object, a specific end, which may be anything at all but which is predetermined in its action and which conditions the agent at the point of departure. Consequently, finality is merely an extension of determinism, and so these two ideas, finality and determinism, are simply two inseparable aspects of one and the same process.

Yet finality takes on different forms according to the nature of the beings concerned. In some (man, for instance) it means that the beings *direct themselves* toward the end by the abstract knowledge that they possess about the relationship between the end and their actions. For example, an instrument made by man's hands is made for a precise purpose; here finality has an explanatory value.

In other beings, not endowed with reason, there is certainly direction to an end toward which they progress. However, they do not know this end explicitly, urged on as they are either by an outer force (a projectile speeds toward its point of impact, predetermined by the power of the explosive used) or by an inner force (as in the case of living things, both plant and animal, but in very different ways). In these two cases of non-rational beings, the end toward which they tend is conditioned by the determinism that explains them: the determinism of the forces of growth for vegetable life, the determinism of purely sensory knowledge and feeling in the animal. In short, here determinism lays down the conditions that create the action and the goal, and that set the goal by directing the acts toward their end. As we shall see in the second part of this chapter, man alone uses his freedom from start to finish.

Thus we can see that, as regards the scientific method, the *utilization* of determinism is the only profitable avenue of exploration. For the goal toward which the structure of a particular living thing tends is not easily perceived. By definition, the end does not exist yet but is in the future, and man alone has the power, by thought, to summon it up before his mind's eye. Moreover, there is also danger that the human observer will endow an animal, for example, with his own psychology and his own aim. Certainly, everything has an aim or object; but in searching for it in biology, one can very easily make mistakes. At most, such an aim will be useful as a provisional hypothesis for a particular organ, but the goal in biology will mostly be seen later, when determinism has worked itself out.

On the other hand, the use of causal physico-chemical determinism deals only with the connection between factors that are past or present and are therefore observable, and thus it gives every guarantee from a scientific point of view. The danger of a generalized use of finality in biology is therefore that it runs the risk of giving an easy, anthropomorphic, and often only verbal explanation.[6] Hence, scientific progress will do well to mistrust it.

It is quite otherwise in the sciences concerning man, where its use is quite natural because here the end is not situated in the future but is present by reason of its being in the human mind. In order to find out who committed a crime, an examining magistrate will first of all try to see if there was a motive that would explain the crime. By the very fact that man himself pursues an aim, an object, by means of the idea which he has formed of it (see above, p. 38), this aim is reflected directly in his behavior, which is largely explained by that aim (as well as by the influence of biological or social determining factors, as we shall see later).

Here also the motive for the "finalist" approach in biology seems to be a desire to find a proof of God's action in the pre-adaptation that it postulates. Certainly this presupposition is not mistaken, but its truth rests on the metaphysical plane and not on that of scientific method. When the scientific method does chart the determined course of some living thing, it is only afterward that the final goal will be seen as such.[7] This is so because, by definition, the scientific method can be used only on things that can be observed, and a goal or aim cannot be observed until it is reached or until it has been rigorously deduced from given fixed data. Thus the point of impact of a projectile can be known only when the projectile strikes or when one has exact knowledge of the factors that have determined its being fired.

2. What Is Life?

We do not propose to speak at length about the inner nature of living things. Instead, our purpose is above all to achieve a climate

---

[6] For example, in the past we have seen it stated in a text book that the reasons ears of wheat have prickles is to keep the birds from stealing the grain! But, then, what about the numerous other kinds of grain crops that do not have such prickles?

[7] Salman, *op. cit.*, p. 406.

in which problems concerning the relationship between science and faith can be raised fairly by eliminating the misunderstandings arising out of ideas that cannot pretend to be traditionally Christian. Hereby we simply wish to clear the ground so that we may be better able to begin the part of this book that is devoted to bringing about the living unity in the believing scientist (chapters four and five). In addition, we shall here attempt only to review certain points that will be helpful toward understanding the second part of this chapter, on human life.

(a) A Description, Not a Definition

From the fact that the precise determining factors of living phenomena still escape the biologist, we must be content with a description of the properties of life instead of looking for a true definition of them. Therefore we must be satisfied with saying that living things are characterized by a complex, graduated organization composed of elements called cells. The matter that goes to make up these cells is further characterized by a special state, the colloidal state, with a predominance of proteids; yet we find in it only bodies that already exist in inert matter. Moreover, in living things there is a perpetual exchange (of matter and energy) between their own structure and their surroundings, and these changes demand very precise conditions both internally and externally (water-based surroundings, atmosphere, temperature, etc.). Finally, living things multiply and reproduce. We can shorten this description and say that living things are marked by the thermodynamic properties of an open irreversible system, with a stationary structure and a minimal tendency to entropy.

(b) Are the Laws of Biology Solely Physico-Chemical?

This question includes the vitalist's attempt to make living things something special, belonging to a domain opposed to that of matter. According to the vitalist, the answer to this question is "No."

But if, following the traditional teaching and the reasoning summarized in the preceding chapter, the universe is divided into matter and spirit, the answer to the question can only be "Yes."

As a matter of fact, the world of the spirit contains: first, God whose action does not follow the same plan as created activity but works in its own special way (as we shall see briefly in the next chapter); secondly, the disembodied intelligences that are known only through faith (the angelic world); and thirdly, the human soul, which is the only active spiritual presence that is perceptible in this world. Consequently all corporeal beings (including the human body itself) are *purely material,* and the laws which God has decreed to govern and explain them can likewise belong only to the material order.

This common sense truth is in harmony with the fundamental discovery of biology that living things contain only elements that exist also in inert matter. Hence we are compelled to conclude that since no spiritual presence is discernible in other living things, as is the case with human reason, their organization and laws must be those of matter, that is to say, physico-chemical in nature.

We had better make one thing clear here. The expression "physico-chemical" is quite vague. If it means the laws that are the object of classical chemistry and physics on the macroscopic scale, then the laws of biology cannot be included therein because of the special qualities of living things. But it is another question if we mean that the laws of biology must be explained by properties that are inherent in matter but that still escape our research. Indeed, this is the direction in which present-day investigations are headed. Some scientists hoped to find the explanation of vital phenomena in the quantum theory, but it seems that they will have to go further.[8]

It is also curious to note that nowadays physicists are often the first to be interested in the problem of the nature of life, in which they find an incentive for their own research.

(c) How, Exactly, Do Living Things Differ from Inert Matter?

In view of what we have just said, it is obvious that we must look for the characteristic qualities of living things in a special organization of inanimate elements, an original structure that makes use of powers that exist at the lower levels of inert matter

---

[8] See A. Goudot, *Les Quanta et la Vie* (Paris, Presses Universitaires de France, 1952), as well as P. Jordan's attempt at an explanation in *La physique et le secret de la vie organique* (Paris, A. Michel, 1959).

but that are used in more complex ways. Hence we can say that living things are composed only of chemical elements that are organized in a special way. Thus, it is a different level of organization; in living things a new level is reached but always with the help of the same materials. However, this does not mean that we can deduce the laws of biology from the laws that govern inert matter, just as we cannot do so for any complex molecule merely by examining the atoms of the substances that compose it. Later, the synthesis reached will explain the link between the two levels of structure. The whole point, therefore, is to attain this synthesis.

It is here that we must connect the nature of living things with what we have already said about the two ways that spirit is present in matter. The mistake of vitalism lies in confusing the two. Apart from the dynamic type of presence attained by the human soul, matter, by the fact that it is intelligible, contains an infinite variety of graduated structures, of ideas embodied in them, one could say. This is even more true of living things, for they have reached a type of organization and they embody ideas that explain their whole being and reveal their origin.

From the fact that a living thing remains itself and maintains its unity during and despite the continual interchange that goes on between it and its surroundings, its organization shows a stability and a dynamic character that are found nowhere else.

Let's take an example. A home owner wants to renovate his house gradually. One year he replaces the roof, another year he does the same with one wall, the next year another wall, and so on for the whole house. After several years his original house has been completely rebuilt but it apparently remains the same because he has replaced the original parts with identical ones, using the same type of brick, the same type of construction, and especially the same floor plan. Materially speaking, the house is not the same anymore. But it is the same as regards the type of structure, general plan and details. If we call this plan the "form" of the house, in the sense in which St. Thomas uses the word "form," we shall be able to say that what characterizes this house, its unity, that which makes it intelligible (intended use, style, etc.) is its "form."

Somewhat the same holds true for living things since their essential characteristic is maintaining the same type of structure despite the incessant interchange (assimilation and elimination) among the materials of which they are made. It is their "form," in the philosophical sense of the word, that characterizes them; that is to say, their own structure persists despite every change. The only difference between the house we mentioned and living things (and it is a big difference) is that in the case of the house, the maintenance of unity and the same type of organization was accomplished by an outside agent, the owner. But living things fill both roles themselves: that of owner and that of the plan of organization.

Speaking about all corporeal beings (apart from man), St. Thomas said that their form (their type of organization as well as the organizing power) comes solely from the possibilities of the matter in which they are actualized. In fact, to use the same comparison as before, the house plan does not exist apart from its incorporation in the materials of the house, through whose agency it shows itself to the attentive observer.

The consequences of this are important. In living things, the unity is clear, since a living thing cannot be divided without being destroyed as a living thing. In living things, the type of organization, the "form," is fully and completely present, both in the whole and in each part of the organism designed in relationship to the whole organism.

This "form," moreover, has a certain immateriality, insofar as it expresses an idea, an intelligible entity. But we must not confuse this with a spiritual principle. Likewise, in a picture painted by an artist, an idea is present embodied in the harmony of the colors. This idea, as an idea, is non-material, but it is material in its realization. Yet we would not therefore say that there is a spiritual principle in the picture. This confusion is a frequent one and is responsible for many misunderstandings.

Perhaps that is so because the very word "principle" is open to confusion. In the spirit of St. Thomas's teaching, "principle" does not mean a real thing but is both a source of explanation, of intelligibility, and a source of being, when it informs any material thing. The only existing reality is the result of this idea, this

structural "form," being embodied in a suitable material.[9] To a
vitalist, on the contrary, "principle" means a mysterious reality,
foreign to the dynamism of the material elements, which do not
draw their capacities from it because the principle is extrinsic to
them. And it is here that the misunderstanding lies, using a vener-
able, traditional term to hide a useless novelty which the materialists are right in rejecting. In man alone this "principle," this
"form" of organization, is more than a principle, because, by virtue
of man's spiritual nature, this form, surpassing the capabilities of
matter, is called subsistent. As a result of an unwarranted trans-
position and under cover of the word "principle," vitalism has
tried to extend man's privilege to all living things.

(d) Life and Consciousness

Until now we have been dealing solely with the general characteristics of living things common to plants and animals, because
the grave misunderstanding that we had to denounce in the name
of Thomistic spiritualism turned upon this point. Having done this,
we are still left with the consideration that if life is not different
from matter, it nevertheless shows an original characteristic in its
more evolved representatives—namely, consciousness or an elementary psychic life, since animals know, suffer, etc. And since
this psychic life approaches so close to man's own psychology,
doesn't it make the vitalists' claim that life is a thing apart a
legitimate one?

If we have understood the distinction between matter and spirit,
we can answer only in the negative. There cannot be a third reality, halfway between matter and spirit. The presence of spirit (in
man) marks a clean break; therefore, everything that is not spirit
is matter. However, the penetration of spirit into matter occurs in
varying degrees, and animals certainly represent the highest degree
of penetration (and indeed in man, this penetration is not merely
an imprint but a true presence). Yet there is a great temptation for
the observer to transpose his own psychology to other animals

---

[9] Evidently, to be more precise, the examples given here with a view to
greater simplicity are concerned with a type of matter that the Thomists
call "secondary" (*materia secunda*), since they have already received a first
determination.

because of the fact that he shares with them an elementary consciousness of a sensible nature.

This animal consciousness is limited to sensory and organic data and is of the same type as they (see the example given in chapter two above, p. 43). However, the animal does elaborate these data in a very complex way; and the great merit of a teaching such as Pavlov's (conditioned reflexes) or of a science such as cybernetics (the science of the techniques of information, of transmission and reactional commands) has truly helped us to understand better the psychology of animals, to see it as a very highly developed servo-motor system with enormous possibilities for receiving information and for bringing together this information through numberless nerve connections and regulatory reactions (feedback effect). There is here a great suppleness of conduct which could give the illusion of true freedom such as man possesses.

This subject deserves to be developed further, yet we do not propose to write a treatise on anthropology but intend mainly to speak out against the misunderstandings that hinder true spiritualism. To put it briefly, the psychological processes of animals bring us to the doors of the spiritual life. Of course, spiritual life cannot come from these processes because it is of a different order, but it finds in them an instrument ready to serve it, as they are developed in human beings.

II. IS MAN FREE?

The preceding pages may have seemed a little argumentative, but it was necessary to recall some distinctions that are too often forgotten and to clarify certain ideas. This clarification will allow us to understand more easily *man's place* in the world of biology and also the *clean break* that he makes with this world of life.

It is in fact these two opposite aspects of human existence that create the greatest difficulty for any attempt to explain it. It is one of the merits of St. Thomas—a merit that is being increasingly emphasized by modern biology—that he safeguarded both man's relationship to the animal world and the irreducible nature of his spiritual being, as well as the vital unity that characterizes him, despite these contradictory demands.

Because this doctrine has often been misunderstood, not to say deformed, since Cartesian dualism, and because it is of great importance to our project, we must now sum it up with some precision.

1. Body and Soul

If we remember the conclusions of the preceding pages, we shall understand that these two realities, body and soul, are not to be regarded under the form of a juxtaposition on the same plane. The unity of the human being would then be illusory. This unity is one of the aspects of human life on which modern science has thrown some penetrating light. In fact all man's actions unfold according to a central and global scheme. The numerous interactions of the physical upon the moral have been minutely detailed and have made possible the birth of psychosomatic medicine. We know, for example, the injurious repercussions of anxiety, worry, and care upon the whole of man's organic life; and the reverse is no less true.

(a) Composition but Not Juxtaposition

The only solution then is to regard this joining of the material and the spiritual in man as a type of composition. However, since compositions can be formed in many different ways, we must be precise as to the only type of composition possible here. What does composition mean in general? It means the making of a new being starting from other beings which lose their individuality in this union. Thus a chemical composition results in a unified body, having stable and precise properties (this is what distinguishes it from a simple mixture, which is only juxtaposition), even to the point where the components disappear in their union and can be found only by analysis.

This type of composition is inconceivable in man because in him matter and spirit do not disappear to produce a third reality different from them both. They could not disappear into each other, anyway, because they are of different kinds and because, for such a union to take place, the elements that are to be fused together must be of the same order. Even in chemistry, the composition of bodies follows the laws of affinity. Matter and spirit are too irreducible to each other, in every aspect that distinguishes the one from the other, to permit us to think of such a composition.

There is therefore only one explanation possible, as shown by our remarks above on life in general. It is that, in man, matter and spirit are joined according to the general plan of the determinant and that which is determined. The materials that go to make up man, all the corporeal and organic elements, find their organization and their specific, unified arrangement under one "form," one idea that they embody and manifest, namely, the form or idea of man. To use the same figure of speech again, the materials that enter into the composition of a house do not have by themselves any disposition to be integrated into the service of such and such type of house, according to such and such plan or architect's idea. So too in man, as in every living thing, the chemical materials that compose him and the forces that they contain, when taken separately, do not have in themselves any determination to be organized in order to become a paramecium, an American beaver, or a twentieth-century Frenchman. Each one of these three beings is made what it is by the organization, the superior structure, that combines these materials in the actual complex edifice.

But for man there is something more: in him there is not only an idea realized in a structure; he is not only "nature," as the modern philosophers will say. He himself is a living idea, a project in progress that assumes its own construction. Spirit is not only present in him (as in every being and especially in every living thing), by a particular mode of organization, a "trace"; but he is himself an *active spirit,* not mere passivity as regards organization (as the bee is urged on inescapably by its instinct), but an activity taking its own nature in hand.

In the second chapter above we have seen this activity at work and the conclusion to which it led us: the presence in man of a spiritual entity that uses and surpasses the material data that come into contact with it through his body.

It is this especially spiritual aspect, that is at once the organization of the material world of man's body and also his independence of matter, that characterizes what we call the "soul." Formerly this word had the more general meaning of "form," and was applicable to every living being, so that one heard about the vegetable soul and the animal soul. But custom has now practically limited this term to man and so we shall use it to mean the *double* function of the soul—that of the "form" of the body and also that of going beyond this role in spiritual activities properly so called. We shall say a few words about these two roles which explain the whole of man.

(b) The Animated Body

Here we must recall what we said about the meaning of the word "principle," to remark that the body and the soul are the principles of the human being. We must not understand thereby two separable things that can exist apart (at least in this world); there exists only the result of their union achieved according to the determined relation (matter) and the determinant (structure or form). Much less must we think of these two principles as a container and what it contains.

My body, throbbing with life, which I touch and sense, is an animated body, organized by the soul. It is the human composite under its corporeal appearance. It is I in my material aspect, a being composed of matter and life. Hence the soul in its organizing function is not external to this body but is *immanent* in it.

Conversely a corpse is no longer a human body. Despite appearances, it is only a collection, a dissociated grouping of organic elements that have lost their original unity to another unity of a subhuman order, namely, those proper to the cycle of putrefaction. Only the temporary maintenance of a purely exterior bodily appearance remains to deceive the observer.

(c) The Human Soul

The essential thing then is to understand that this soul—which animates the body, which is the organizing element in the human being, and which explains his corporeal life in terms of a general class (that of the animals)—is the same soul that, going beyond this strictly biological function, displays an activity that is proper to it, by a total independence of matter in its strictly spiritual operations.

Some important consequences flow from this. First, since it is the same soul that is both the organizing principle of the body (the "form") and also a spiritual being itself, the complete unity of man is safeguarded. Some may perhaps object and ask how a spiritual reality can have an organic function. This objection has often been made in the course of history and is the result of a complete misunderstanding of the relationships between matter and spirit. If these two realities are regarded as two worlds completely separated from each other (radical dualism) the objection is fully justified. But remember what we said above about the two ways that spirit can be present in matter. Even lifeless matter (and hence much more so living matter) possesses a structure and has a nature or a type of being, only by reason of an idea embodied in it, which it shows passively. *A fortiori*, then, the spirit can exist as an active idea, a real presence, in matter. If we have understood that the whole role of matter is to be penetrated by spirit and determined by it (and that is what makes matter intelligible), it is easy to see that matter can be penetrated more fully in man. Matter is then put at the service of a type of spiritual being and is actively animated by it. It does not possess just an inert trace of spiritual being, but is taken into active participation with it. That is one profound reason for the dignity of the human body. This doctrine, then, could not be more favorable to the efforts of modern science in its research into the interdependence of organic functions and those of the soul.

However, we must be on our guard against looking upon this dependence as the result of an emanation. The soul is certainly dependent upon the body for its functions as a whole. But because of its spirituality, its different nature, it cannot emanate from matter, for it belongs to an order, a world, that is absolutely "other." That is what the metaphysical materialist cannot understand, and so he views the soul as being a product of the body. For instance, Taine declared that "thought is secreted by the brain as bile is by the liver"; and according to Lenin, "Materialism consists in holding that the spirit has no existence independent of the body, for the soul is only a secondary factor, a function of the brain." [10] But the brain is only an organ at the service of spiritual thought, albeit an indispensable organ, and the extraordinary complexity of sense

[10] See V. Lenin, *Materialism and Empirio-criticism* (Collected Works, Vol. XIII [New York, International Publishers Co., Inc.]).

images of which it is capable because of the millions of neurons that compose it makes it eminently suitable for this role.

Conversely, we must not think, along the lines of Descartes and so many naive spiritualists, that man is only a spiritual soul which, despite its union with the body, has an independent existence, coming from outside to animate an animal body (e.g., Descartes' example of the rider and his horse).

Rather, *man is both an animal in his whole being* (and this animality penetrates to his purely spiritual functions, giving them a special "coloring") and *a spirit in his whole being* (and this spirituality also penetrates to his purely organic functions). St. Thomas expressed this truth by saying that rationality (or spirituality) and animality are related to each other as the determinant to the determined. Generically man is an animal, and specifically a spiritual being (a rational animal).

These considerations are of prime importance for a proper understanding of religion and of the distinctively human character it must take on if it is to remain authentic. In God's presence man must never forget the basic duality that places him on the frontier of two worlds, and he must also remember that in his human nature he joins them in a union that does not eliminate their specific differences. This should be the foundation of his religious attitude, of the style it must assume, and of the responsibility he must undertake.[11]

Secondly, because the soul is a "form," its active organizing presence is seen everywhere. Therefore, the soul is at once in every part of the body, whole and entire in the body as a whole. Its spirituality accentuates the impossibility of localizing it, as well as its independence of materializing conditions.

Therefore, we cannot say that the soul is contained in the body as in a receptacle or a prison, because it is present throughout the body, both as the idea that presides over all the details of an architectural whole, and as the architect who is everywhere present, not exterior to the work, but immanent in it. Hence we see

[11] In this regard, the expression "I have a soul" is not exactly correct. We do not possess our souls, which belong to the domain of being rather than to that of possessions, to use G. Marcel's phrase. It would be more correct to say "I am a soul, just as I am a body," for these are two aspects of the same reality, the first of which explains the second.

how ridiculous it was for the biologists of the last century to refuse to believe in the soul because they had never found it with their scalpels. This is exactly the same as if a mechanic refused to believe in the idea that explained the motor that he was taking apart because he never found it under his screwdriver.[12] Descartes placed the soul in the pineal gland because he refused to grant the soul this relationship with the body.

Since it is present throughout the body, the soul puts the mark of spirituality on all man's actions, even those that come from his animal nature. There is a human way of eating, drinking, loving, etc., that, for the close observer, bears the stamp of the spiritual because of a certain independence of matter in its mode of action. This spiritual presence shows itself at all stages of man's organic life—his bearing, fingerprints, voice, facial expression, and especially language. This fact is at the basis of techniques like graphology and physiognomy.[13]

But it is obviously in its own sphere, in strictly human activities, that the spiritual shows itself. Thus, in chapter two we were able to use the fact of rational knowledge to find out the order to which the source of this knowledge belonged. We should remark that this "emerging" activity, while truly spiritual, is not thereby disembodied and isolated from everything else. It can take place only by exploiting and using all those functions that are, strictly speaking,

[12] This is the same narrowness of outlook which the Soviet propagandists showed when they exploited their cosmonauts' flight by stating (quite seriously) that Titov and Gagarin had seen neither God nor angels in outer space.

[13] On this subject we should note that there are in current usage some confused expressions that can be applied to the two facets of the soul's activities, the animal and the spiritual. The word "love" is an example. In order to see if love is at the human level, one must find out whether or not it is based upon spiritual values above the element of passion, upon the dignity of the person loved and his or her own good. How many people think that they are in love, when in reality they love only themselves in the other person because of the pleasure the other gives them! And since this pleasure quickly fades (as does everything organic), their supposedly "eternal" love vanishes because it does not come from a more profound source.

It is much the same with other words and phrases like "psychological life" or "intelligence" which are applied indiscriminately to humans and to animals. The careful observer will be alert to see the break demanded by the difference between the spiritual and the organic.

organic, corporeal and common to the whole animal world, as an instrument by which the soul achieves effects of which it would be incapable by itself.

That is the reason why, in man, spiritual activity is marked by a weakness that has led some people to think that the body is a prison for the soul (cf. Plato's mythical cave and Lamartine's "fallen god"). But the ambiguity of man's condition is simply explained by an *instrumental dependence;* he can only live the life of the spirit in this world under the conditions imposed by the matter in which he is plunged by his body.

(d) The Psychological Life of Men and Animals

We have already alluded to the psychological life of animals, which is a sort of complex servo-motor system. In man, this psychological life obviously exists as a basis for his life as a man and as an instrument of his activity, an activity that demonstrates its spirituality in the way it uses this instrument. We have also seen that man, knowing universal concepts by his reason, can meet myriad situations and envisage very different implementations of the same idea. Immersed though he is in the world, in historical, concrete situations, he still can go beyond his environment by rational abstraction to conceive a project or try to change his situation. He can do this because the ideas which his reason attains can be more or less abstract. Some of these ideas, the higher ones, are generic in nature and hence allow of a great variety of implementations or specifications, some even being the opposite of others.

Because of this man can discover and even create, if necessary, a scale of appreciation. Hence, he has access to what psychologists call the world of "values" (the meaning to be given to a situation, or a hard fact, as we shall see later in connection with the freedom of the will). This insertion of the spiritual into man's animal psychological life explains the infinite adaptability, the independence of surroundings, and the tendency toward progress that are so characteristic of human conduct. As Claudel puts it: "The animal is made to exist in a certain environment, but man is born to make his way everywhere."

2. The Human Person

The human soul is independent of the material world which, however, impinges on it through the medium of the body. This soul, which is the organizing element and the "form" of man, makes him a being absolutely unique in the universe. Closely bound up with the cosmos, a being-in-the-world, he is nevertheless able to stand back from it, to look straight at it, even to become master of it, that is to say, to take it over and shape it to his plans.

This is the basic reason for scientific progress. Animals are confined to a certain mode of sense life. They cannot make progress to a higher plane because they are prisoners of the needs of the present or of the instinct of their species. The human soul, on the contrary, demonstrates its spirituality by its wish for independence, for unceasing progress, and it is never satisfied, never appeased. The mere possibility of asking oneself the question "Has man a soul?" proves that the soul exists. The soul is nothing other than this typically human center of action opening out upon the infinity of the world, but able to be independent of it, and capable of looking at itself while asking such questions.

(a) Independence

Man's independence, because of the spirituality of his soul, is expressed by the term "person," which therefore designates the spiritual being that functions in and through the body. Now we know that the spirit is by definition an intelligible plenitude, an autonomous existence to a supreme degree. Only through it can matter say anything to us, or reply to our questions.

We can therefore see that it is not a question of spirit's passive participation in matter but of the spirit itself as an active, animating center, culminating in an autonomous sphere; for the spirit that is the human person has within it an interior richness that puts it outside any category. A person therefore cannot be an object, a thing, a passive nature that can be classified, for he transcends that order of being. That is why he can never become the property of anyone else and can never be reached intimately except by an inner encounter and especially by an act of love. Furthermore, this inner nature of persons often makes it difficult for them to have an exchange or a true communication between them. Only a communion at their source, God, the pure Spirit, will permit such an exchange. In short, each human person is a unique, irreplaceable entity, whence comes his great dignity.

(b) Survival and Immortality

Let us now examine this entity more closely. The person soon appears as engaged in a destiny, a history. And how is this? We can see it in the reply to the question, "Is the human soul immortal?"

Since the idea of mortality is directly accessible to us, it would be better to ask, "Is the soul *mortal?*" It is therefore enough to see if the idea of mortality can be realized in the soul according to what we know about the soul.

What is death? It is not an annihilation (nothing is lost and nothing is created, at least on the macroscopic scale); it is essentially a dissociation, the loss of a unity. If I break a beautiful vase into many pieces I can say that it is dead, although quantitatively nothing has disappeared and not one of the pieces has been annihilated. If I kill a rabbit its death does not result from any loss of matter; only the unstable balance of its functions, that is to say, its "form" or organizing element, has disappeared. This "form" is dead just as the beautiful geometric form of the vase is dead, both of them being two very different ideas incarnated in matter so that once their unity has disappeared only the dissociated matter remains. We see, then, that if something is to die, it must be divisible, it must have parts that can be dissociated; and this is obviously true of the human body.

The human soul, on the contrary, is not material, does not come under the domain of quantity and extension, and therefore is not divisible. There is no possibility that it will lose a unity that results only from an assembly of parts. It is obvious that the geometric form of the vase and the structural and organizing form of the rabbit have disappeared because of their union with matter and their dependence on its fate, on the fragile unity that they manifested.

Because of its spirituality, its independence of the corporeal world, the human soul is called "simple," i.e., not composed of parts, although it does form a composite with the body to make up the whole man. And since it is not a composite, it is not divisible and cannot be destroyed. Death cannot affect it, and it survives the dissolution of the body.

Hence, holding that the soul is immortal, that it subsists after the death of the body, is not the result of a blind belief, a groundless assumption, but is rather a reasonable recognition of a fact. Then what does happen to the soul? This raises the whole problem of man's destiny. What is the meaning of this destiny? How can we make this meaning more precise? If we retain our analytical outlook, we can suspect that the nature of man's destiny can be discovered to some extent from an examination of the deep, typical tendencies of human psychological life. Obviously, while we are doing this, we can be concerned only with a destiny toward which the soul tends naturally—not that which could be offered to it and which we shall discuss in chapter five. An analysis of human freedom will afford us an avenue of approach to the goal toward which man tends and upon which the survival of his soul opens up a unique perspective.

3. Freedom

(a) Under Pressure

We could doubt that man is free when we reflect upon the various pressures that are exerted upon him and that often explain his conduct.

First of all there are personal, biological factors, which can be summed up as the influence of the unconscious upon human life. Psychoanalysis teaches that there exists in man a whole lower, unconscious life which has its own laws and which can influence us strongly by many motivations. These, although apparently free, are explained by uncontrollable impulses and suggestions coming from the depths of our being. One of the merits of existentialism has been to denounce the excess of this explanation. Our psychological consciousness bears witness that in many circumstances we are certain that we completely dominate biological factors, after many hesitations and much vacillation. Far from being irresistibly urged on by the power of a determining motive while being left with the illusion that we are freely choosing our course of action, in reality it is our own free decision that gives the seemingly determining motive its own weight and value.

Now, some may say that it is not only biological conditions that urge man onward but also the whole social atmosphere in which he lives. Indeed, social constraint does act powerfully on human psychological reactions (education, current fashions, advertising, conformism, etc.). Moreover, man does not act the same way in society as he would in a state of isolation. Here too we must acknowledge the importance of determining factors which rule many of our actions. But a closer examination quickly shows that they do not destroy our freedom. They do *limit* it, and confine it to more restricted choices and areas, but man, because of his spiritual soul, can transcend his surroundings or even repudiate them by an act of detachment. Or, on the contrary, he can accept them, even if he may give the impression of being shaped by them.

(b) What, Then, Is Freedom?

Let us first see what freedom is not, by examining the true nature of that pseudo-freedom which, basically, is the only one accepted by the critics of psychological or social determinism.

Many make freedom consist in the absence of constraint, in the sense that a wild animal is free. This is called *physical* freedom, which is not proper to man alone but belongs to every animal that is left to itself. This freedom is therefore the expression of spontaneity. If we limited freedom to this meaning, then the objections given above would be fully justified. A wild animal seems to be free from external constraint but this is only apparent. The animal does not do what it wants to do, for it is the slave of its racial instinct and its surroundings and is unable to resist their urgings. For many men who are the slaves of tyrannical habits, freedom is limited to this caricature.

Furthermore, we must point out that there's a perpetual temptation to abdicate before the demands of true inner freedom and to foster the illusion that we continue to be free because we are not in chains. The dehumanization brought about by the mechanization of modern life, the inner emptiness of so many souls, the disregard for spiritual things, the power of propaganda—all these, even outside of totalitarian regimes, contribute to making us vulnerable to the forces of social pressure and blind instincts. Then there is the flight from responsibility, the search for a deceptive security in the anonymity of the crowd. That is the abdication of freedom.

What, then, is true freedom? It is the affirmation of the superiority of the spirit over matter. In order to assert itself more firmly and to be sure of its own authenticity, this moral and spiritual freedom often chooses to renounce physical freedom. That is, for example, what the cloistered religious does when, no longer possessing physical freedom, he enjoys to the full his inner freedom. Although he is confined to the cloister, he has chosen to be so, overcoming the instincts that urge him to live a social or family life. He has sacrificed his physical freedom in order to affirm more strongly his moral independence and in order to have more direct access to the realm of the spirit. In the same way the political prisoner, incarcerated because he has chosen to be faithful to an ideal, is behind bars because he wishes to be and because he prefers this fate to an outer freedom that would be a moral constraint. Thus we can say that in his cell he is more free than his jailer, who is a docile servant of the regime that employs him.

On the contrary, the adolescent, who rejects every rule and wants to lead what he thinks is a free life, runs the risk of becoming disillusioned. He can withdraw from social or family pressures, but these are only external restraints. Actually he is in danger of falling into greater bondage to his unbridled instincts, and despite appearances he will not really have attained freedom.

(c) The Source of Freedom

How are we to form a true idea of this freedom which seems to be opposed to the principle of determinism that is so universal?

There is, first of all, one explanation that must be rejected as entirely inadequate, although it has been defended by great minds, such as Eddington, and has been widely used as a sheet-anchor by many spiritualists who are not much concerned about the demands of philosophy. This explanation simply links human free will with the indeterminist interpretation of the quantum theory.[14] Thus the proponents of this theory try to find the source of human free will in the relationships of uncertainty discovered by Heisenberg (the impossibility of pinpointing and foreseeing with certainty the positions and speeds of elementary corpuscles).

But freedom is not to be sought at this sub-atomic level. Its root is elsewhere, eluding the grasp of any scientific critique, for it is in *the very structure of the human soul,* and belongs to an eminently spiritual order of being, as we shall try to show.

We have seen that man's affective polarity is manifested on the spiritual level by the autonomy of his will, his power of spontaneity that transcends the world of sense. Now the will, since it tends toward an object, toward a good to be attained, thereby presupposes that that object, that concrete good, has been presented to it by the power of thought operating on the same level as itself. We have also seen that this thought, while seeing an object in its act of knowing, sees in that object, that thing, the realization of an idea, of a general type, surpassing its material embodiment. Of course, the senses and emotions show this object as a good in the sensory order, but if man acts as man, he does not allow himself to be determined by this sensory attraction. He weighs the pros and cons to determine whether or not this object corresponds to the idea that he is pursuing, and he always finds a disproportion between the concrete object and the idea because of the innate disparity between the two which comes from their

[14] Obviously, materialists reacted violently against this explanation and the true spiritualist will do so too. See, for example, Bertrand Russell, *The Scientific Outlook,* (New York, N. W. Norton & Company, Inc., 1931), pp. 97f.; or M. Boll: "Heisenberg's discovery has been made the pretext for an exultant shout of conquest, a victory parade, over the supposed ruins of the scientific concept of the world which had been accused of having sinned against the spirit. . . . All the spiritualists, who have been champing at the bit for two or three generations, have thrown themselves on this heavenly manna" (*Les quatre faces de la Physique* [Paris, 1939] pp. 242f.). The responsibility of those spiritualists who were misled by this confusion is clear. A good summation is given by A. Metz, "Causalité scientifique et causalité première," in *Archives de Philosophie* (July-December, 1961), pp. 517ff., especially p. 531.

different natures.[15] He will not be irresistibly drawn on; he will always be able to dream of a better and more ideal embodiment of the idea. From childhood to old age this disparity between the dream and the reality reveals a tendency of man's whole psychological life. If he is not free of an ideal of happiness, of development, that urges him to search everywhere for its attainment, by that very fact he remains free of all other concrete, sensory things that are offered to him but always leave him unsatisfied because of their very finiteness and imperfection.

Further, we must note that biological or sociological determining factors will very often have a role to play in limiting this choice and reducing the disparity. But if the prize is worth striving for, if man feels that the decision is a grave one, he is conscious of his responsibility for his choice and he will override the determinants in complete independence, and will exert himself to make a truly free choice. Indeed, certain critical situations will put his freedom to a severe test, namely, when he must make a choice in the face of a piercing temptation or a tormenting sensory allurement. The will's power of resistance and its adherence to an ideal that it has glimpsed is then the true measure and the real image of its freedom.

Human freedom, then, is an affirmation of independence made possible by the spirituality of the soul. Human reason, being able to abstract and envisage general ideas, can give meaning to a situation, to a hard fact. For example, a man is killed by a bullet from a revolver. The physicist will trace the trajectory of the bullet, its penetrating force, and its effect. The biologist will see in the dead man the arresting of his vital metabolism, etc. But the man's death has a meaning, and it may even have several. It may be a crime, a legitimate act of self-defense, or an act of heroism. In a word, it has some "value." But that only means that it can be viewed as an example of a species under a generic idea that is

15 For example, I have to buy a car, and I form an idea of what I like and need. When the salesmen show me many different models, I am equally attracted by several, for I see in some the qualities or the defects that are lacking in others, etc. In the face of the disparity between the ideal car (which really doesn't exist) and the actual cars on sale, I shall remain free to choose, and I shall not be irresistibly drawn to any particular car.

taken as a norm (e.g., the idea of rights—the rights of the individual or of society—and the different possible relationships between
these two ideas, explain how one can discuss the lawfulness or
unlawfulness of the death penalty).

And since ideas attained by the spirit are more or less complex
(whether generic or specific), the implications of a particular situation can be quite varied. They are ranked in relationship to a very
general idea that acts as a standard according to which the values
will be judged. For example, eating a certain dish seems good to
me; but if I abstain from eating it, it may be because I want to
avoid a possible stomach ache or, on the contrary, because I want
to practice self-discipline and mortify myself. The ranking of
values, which is the expression of freedom, is therefore a function
of an abstract ideal of a generic nature, that is, of a spiritual
nature.

Thus man gives a value, a meaning, to facts and situations
above and beyond their determinant features; these features, however, are not destroyed by free will. On the contrary, freedom
integrates them by giving them a meaning, either to restrain them
or to assume them; and in doing this free will does a spiritual
work.[16]

4. Conclusion

This opening of the human spirit upon a boundless horizon,
discovered by its spiritual thought, causes it constantly to insert
into the heart of its desires the nostalgia for an ideal of a limitless
happiness and expansion. This spiritual urge starts man out on a
breathless race toward a better existence that always recedes before him; it leaves him with the dissatisfaction that results from the
possession of limited, passing things in which he momentarily believes he has found repose. Human freedom is constantly concerned with this dialectic of disproportion, a disproportion which
explains scientific progress and the rise of civilization, the ceaseless
search for new modes of life capable of bringing greater happiness.

[16] We can see, then, how Lenin could say that the Marxist regime had
nothing to do with freedom.

Yet man's sadness or disenchantment (or the anguish so well described by existentialism) shows that the human heart, hearing the call of the infinite in the voice of its thought, is not made to find, in all these things that surround it and that seduce it for a moment, the haven in which it can rest.

Man's survival in his spiritual being is therefore a precious indication confirming the strangeness of his earthly situation in relationship to the other things of nature. He is not really made to settle down among them once and for all. Is not his destiny, then, an encounter, in the midst of his earthly tasks, with a reality for which he was made and whose call he hears as he struggles to reach the truth in his research?

That is what we must now examine in the second part of this book.

PART TWO

ACHIEVING UNITY

We are now at the heart of our project—the union between the life of science and the life of faith. This union must be accomplished at that common source of which these two lives partake in different degrees.

The ground has been prepared by the foregoing chapters. They have shown us the path we must follow, the way whereby we must approach the divine mystery, starting from its relationship with the structure of the universe and of man.

Since our aim is not to write apologetics, we shall not set down in order the proofs for the existence of God; moreover, it would be ridiculous to try to summarize these proofs in a few pages. Yet we must be clear on the meaning of an approach to God, that is, of a more profound realization of what he should represent to a scientist and from what angle we should attempt such an approach.

In the next two chapters we shall deal first with finding God in his created work, which the scientist makes the object of his research, and secondly with a deepening of this encounter with God's uncreated work, in his Son. In our last chapter we shall give a concrete example of the union we are seeking.

IV
FINDING GOD
IN CREATION

A basic question immediately arises, one that concerns our whole project—namely, is there a problem as regards God? And by what means can we hope to attempt our approach to and meeting with him?

When we have answered this question, we can sketch out a path toward the divine mystery, starting from natural elements that are at the scientist's disposal. We can then perhaps better understand the relationship between God and the world, and can ascertain the part that man's work plays in the divine plan.

I. TO WHAT ORDER DOES THE PROBLEM OF GOD BELONG?

The worst mistake we could make in considering this question would be to tackle it as if it were a human or natural problem. In fact, we cannot conceive our approach to God as merely a dialectical extension of the one that has occupied us until now. Once we wish to fix our eyes on the reality whose existence we have ascertained through our earlier efforts, a clean break must be made because we shall certainly not discover the inner nature of that reality by the power of pure reason.

1. A Problem of Limits

What do we actually mean by the word "God"? He is by definition the Being that cannot be measured by anything and who, on the contrary, is the measure of everything. Of course, when human thought finds in created things the marks or signs of a spiritual presence (as we have seen in the preceding chapters), it can trace their intelligibility back to a higher principle of explanation, the source of everything. But how are we to begin to understand this source itself?

In other words, rationalism's great mistake is to try to make God just one object among all others, on the same plane as they. An object is that which confronts the mind, that can be understood, that is, brought up to a higher category. Now, if by God we mean the Being that creates all other beings, he obviously cannot enter a category above himself. This would be begging the question. He cannot be reached in himself because by definition one cannot refer him back to anything other than himself.

Thus wanting to know God is to acknowledge at the outset a total incapacity for understanding him by human reasoning. Our encounter with him must begin with the realization that our human techniques of knowledge are insufficient here. Our acceptance of this insufficiency is the very condition for a possible entrance to the divine mystery. In short, knowing God is not a problem like other problems; it is a problem of the limits of human thought. It would simply be ridiculous to attempt to reach God's inner nature, to say what he is.

But it's quite another question when we are dealing, not with God's inner nature, but with his existence and with what we can call his external nature, as it appears "from outside." Although I may not be able to look directly at the blazing sun, yet I can feel its heat and investigate its nature. While God's inner life is concealed from us, we can know of his existence as shown by the dependence of the universe on him. The problem here, however, is something quite different. Since we have acknowledged the limitations of our ability to know God in himself, we are by this very fact in the state of mind required to encounter him as he is reflected in his creation.

2. Psychological Conditions for This Encounter

Therefore, we can be concerned here only with finding God in the traces he has left in the cosmos, a task for which our minds are equipped. However, we must take certain precautions.

Our efforts at reasoning during our search must be exerted in a psychological context, keeping in mind the whole man, if we do not wish to come to a dead end. What, in fact, are we trying to do? We want to find out whether or not God exists: i.e., we want to answer a question whose dimensions go beyond those questions we can ask about the existence of other beings. Even apart from our search, God is by definition the source of all beings, including ourselves. He is the Being from whom we receive everything and to whom we are indebted for all that we are.

Hence, to pose the question of the existence of God is to pose the most important question for every intelligent man, the one question which has a bearing on the whole of life. For if the answer is in the negative, the world and our existence are absurd (see the end of this chapter); but if it is in the affirmative, we must take account of it in our lives, perhaps changing or even revolutionizing them. And an answer can be given only when we appreciate the gravity of the choice and when we feel vitally concerned about the nature of the response. Again, such a question simply cannot be approached like any other (for example in a pretentiously intellectual discussion at a cocktail party).

Let us use a metaphor which, though awkward, is still instructive. A bomb-like device has been found in a vacant lot and no one knows whether it is a hoax or the real thing. An explosives expert is called in to disarm it and he too asks himself the question, "Is it a real bomb or not?" He considers the matter very carefully because his own life is in great danger if he does not seriously take into account the possibility that the device really is a bomb. He can't afford to treat the whole thing as a joke; the risk is too great for that. It is somewhat the same with the question of the existence of God, for the answer can affect the whole of one's life.

3. What Means Are We To Employ?

What means have we at our disposal to begin answering this essential question?

Let us immediately state that these means *absolutely cannot be of the same order as scientific method or explanation.* Science begins with observable phenomena and remains within the domain of measurable things. Even when its study results in an abstract relationship, that relationship is always in reference to a "phenomenal" aspect. Hence, God cannot be detected at this scientific conceptual level. However, this does not mean to say that he is not found there in some fashion (as we shall see later); he is present even there in material objects, which bear the traces of his passing. He can be truly discovered only by appealing to a method other than that of the logico-mathematical method of science.

Indeed, if we remain on the plane of scientific explanation, our answer must be on the same plane. We have seen that the great temptation of anthropomorphism has always been to presuppose that there exists, on the same level as material phenomena, a mysterious spiritual reality that has the duty of explaining these phenomena. Thus, in the Middle Ages people believed that God had his angels rotate the celestial crystal spheres. And even yet, for many people in the modern world, God is the immediate source of life for every living thing through the medium of a mysterious vital principle. This is a kind of primitive mentality that sees behind every natural phenomenon a closely allied mysterious presence on the same level. The result can only be to produce "a false god, or, in other words, an idol." [1]

Yet, the technical data (though not the technique itself) can be legitimately employed in the development of the classical proofs for the existence of God, as Pope Pius XII pointed out in a well-known speech. [2] It is only necesssary to mark out the limits within which such technical data should be used. They should be employed merely to clarify and broaden our knowledge of the starting points of these proofs, which, by definition, are based on human experience.

And what light should guide us in our search, on the natural level? Simply the humblest and at the same time the most human light—that which comes from the spontaneous use of our reason, from simple common sense to philosophical conclusions.

---

[1] H. Paissac, "Preuves de Dieu" in *Lumière et Vie* No. 14 (1954), p. 90.
[2] Allocution to the Pontifical Academy of Sciences, November 22, 1951, on the proofs for the existence of God in the light of modern natural sciences.

Does this mean that one must be a professional philosopher
or metaphysician in order to begin this undertaking properly? That
would be too much to ask. Besides, in every layman as in every
scientist there is a spontaneous use of natural reason, a true philosophy, though often unconscious and unformulated.[3]

In fact, it is impossible for the human mind not to ask itself
certain questions of a general nature. And the scientist who leaves
his laboratory well pleased with his discoveries can very well realize that his own research often goes beyond the path it normally
follows and may even contract grave responsibilities.[4]

From the moment a person forms any opinion about the meaning of his life or his work, or adopts an outlook on the world
and man's role in it, he has a philosophy. It is true that many
scientists have no great esteem for philosophy, often with good

[3] "An undiscussed background of philosophy is often the scientist's haven
of rest. He thinks that his philosophy is a summary of his knowledge but
often it is only the first beginnings of his knowledge, a condensation of the
first interests that urged him on toward that knowledge. The scientist does
not even always profess the clear-sighted philosophy of his own science.
Science does not possess the philosophy that it deserves." (Bachelard, *Le
Matérialisme rationnel*, [Presses Universitaires de France, 1953], p. 20).
One of the great modern physicists has written in the same vein: "In
developing itself, science is necessarily led to introduce into its theories
concepts that have a philosophical meaning, such as time, space, objectivity,
causality, individuality, etc. . . . Science tries to give these concepts precise
definitions in respect to the methods that it uses, but it tries to avoid all
philosophical discussion about them. Perhaps, in acting thus science often
uses metaphysics without knowing it, which is not the least dangerous way
of doing it." (L. de Broglie, "Le Mathématicien au seuil de la Métaphysique," *Revue de Métaphysique et Morale*, 1947, p. 321.)

[4] This was the case with the scientists who worked on the development
of the atomic bomb. When they realized the repercussions of their research
on the future of mankind "some of them almost lost their minds, while
others showed such moral instability that they were involved in some
amazing brushes with the law. These reactions meant that the scientists in
question discovered the existence of metaphysics under the appearance of a
concrete particularly striking case." (G. Gusdorf, *Traité de Métaphysique*
[Colin, 1956] p. 97). Thus we can say that science, having reached its
present stage and by reason of its advances (see chapter one above), is
opening out on to a vaster form of thought, and that it actually has a
responsibility to do so. "Science thus leads to the burning shores of metaphysics." (P. Vendryes, *L'acquisition de la Science* [Paris, A. Michel, 1946],
p. 446).

reason.[5] But although the scientist distrusts philosophy, he must not refuse to lay aside his scientific methods of thought in order to tackle the problem of God's existence. He does not use scientific methods in other important decisions in his life, such as choosing a wife, joining a political party, etc., where he uses his natural reason like any ordinary man. Moreover, knowing whether or not God exists is something so vital and important that the answer cannot be inaccessible to human reason unaided by any specialized technique, although man must be willing to mitigate somewhat the rigor of his logic.

In short, although science as such cannot prove that God exists, the scientist is nonetheless a man and, by using the lessons he has learned from experience, he can exercise his reason critically in trying to find an answer to this eternal question.[6]

II. THE EXISTENCE OF GOD

Following St. Thomas, Catholic philosophers have gathered together in a doctrinal system five ways of reaching the existence of

[5] Modern philosophy, particularly existentialism, is little interested in the problems posed by science, and scientists are shocked when they see the ignorance that many philosophers display when they discuss scientific problems. In addition, a scientist such as Oppenheimer is able to state that the philosophy of scientists, insofar as they have one, is completely out of date and totally unsuited to modern times. (Cf. *Bulletin de l'Union catholique des scientifiques français,* September-October, 1957, p. 51.) Teilhard de Chardin wrote in like manner: "I cannot understand how a man can call himself a phenomenologist and write whole books without even mentioning cosmogenesis and evolution! Truly, Sartre and Merleau-Ponty (and the other philosophers at the Sorbonne) are still living in a pre-Galilean universe." (Letter of April 11, 1953; see *La Table ronde,* June, 1953, p. 39).

[6] Just because science cannot prove the existence of God, we must not conclude that science is atheistic, as certain spiritualists do. The word "atheistic" is very ambiguous. To the ordinary man it means "denying the existence of God." But science does not have to prove or disprove his existence because the question is outside its province. Science is no more atheistic than art or human labor. Like these things, it can provide a point of departure for an ascent to God, but the actual ascent itself is of another order—the reflective exercise of natural reason. The use of this ambiguous word ("atheistic") is an example of the confused thinking of some philosophers, in blatant contrast to the vigorous logic demanded in scientific circles.

God. While these ways have different origins and their starting points vary, they do have one characteristic in common—they all ascend to God starting from the vestiges and traces of his action that he has left in the world of matter and in man. Obviously, in the course of time, these ways have been elaborated, discussed, and called into question. In our day, some people are asking how useful they are to the modern mind.[7] From time to time, they might simply be revised, or new light might be thrown on them, for the basic intuition they contain certainly has a permanent value.

This is not the place, however, to review them, for our aim is more modest. We are speaking especially to scientists, and, as an extension of the reasoning process set down in detail in the preceding chapters, we shall try to make use of some of the elements in some of these "ways" (especially the fourth and fifth) that refer to the intelligibility of the world.

1. Starting Point: The Intelligibility of the Universe

Einstein's remark is well known: "One may say 'the eternal mystery of the world is its comprehensibility.' " [8] This is echoed by Louis de Broglie: "The great wonder in the progress of science is that it has shown us that there is a certain agreement between our thought and things—a possibility that, with the help of the resources of our intelligence and the rules of our reason, we can grasp the profound relationships existing between phenomena. We are not surprised enough by the fact that any science is possible for us: that is to say, that our reason gives us the means to understand at least certain aspects of what is happening around us in nature." [9]

These reflections clearly show that the most profound truths are often the most commonplace ones, so much so that pointing them out may cause surprise because they appear to be so simple and to

[7] On this point, see C. Tresmontant, *Toward the Knowledge of God* (Baltimore, The Helicon Press, Inc., 1961), and especially F. van Steenberghen, *Dieu caché* (Louvain, Nauwelaerts, 1961).

[8] A. Einstein, *Out of My Later Years* (New York, Philosophical Library Inc., 1950), p. 61.

[9] L. de Broglie, *Physique et Microphysique* (Paris, A. Michel, 1947), pp. 229-230.

present no problem. But the mark of the true scientific spirit is this capacity to wonder at the most ordinary things and to retain enough freshness of outlook to discern their hidden strangeness. The path that allows us to approach God is of this type.

What is the significance of this fact referred to by two modern scientific experts? It poses one of the most fundamental problems: *Why can human thought say something about the world that confronts it?* How can thought discover the meaning of the world and enunciate the laws that govern it? The answer to this question, which is already contained essentially in what we have written so far, can be formulated gradually in the following stages:

2. First: The Intelligibility of the World Was Not Created by Man

The intelligibility of the world could be regarded as basically the result of man's efforts, his expression of reality in concepts. Certainly the formulation of the laws of science is the product of man's mind, but no scientist doubts for a moment that they express only a part of reality, that they are only a way to "nibble at it," as it were.

If the research worker doubted for a moment that the results of his research had real significance or suspected that they were the purely subjective product of his thought, a sort of inner rumination without any real importance, the very reason for his work would vanish. If the scientist toils and labors, struggling with matter that eludes him, it is to wrench its secrets from it, to dominate it by penetrating it with his mind.

Obviously, this conviction of the scientist presupposes that the universe is intelligible in itself even before the human mind investigates and penetrates it. This intelligibility was not created by man's coming into contact with the world; the world, having the innate capacity for being thought of and understood, possessed it beforehand. We have sufficiently developed this characteristic of the material universe so that there is no need to stress it further here (see chapter two above).

Thus, at the heart of matter and of all beings that are the objects of science, there is an intelligible structure, an objective content, that can be seized by the human mind, to which it reveals itself as an answer to the mind's search.

3. Second: This Intelligibility Is Spiritual in Nature

At this point we must get a clear idea of the nature of this intelligibility. It is obviously similar in kind to human thought. In fact, unless we wish to fall into the error of idealism by denying the independent existence of the world of matter—a denial that a scientist cannot make—we must acknowledge that there is a certain likeness, proportion or relationship between reality and human thought. If the universe were absolutely different from us, if there were nothing in common between it and human thought, then every attempt at penetrating it intellectually would be doomed to failure. The whole of scientific progress gets its most powerful impetus from this profound conviction. To take just one example, isn't the harnessing of nuclear energy the strongest confirmation that scientific thought has grasped the structure of reality?

We can say, therefore, that the intelligibility of matter seems to be of the same kind as the structure of the human mind. All scientific truth and progress are founded on this likeness, this secret relationship between what matter reveals and what man seeks in it. Consequently, the same reality that constitutes the human mind (and which, in all its characteristics, is different from matter) also constitutes, under another form, the intelligible aspect of matter. Moreover, it is this likeness that allows man to superimpose his own structure upon that of matter by means of scientific techniques.

These two kinds of structure, the one that matter possesses of itself and the one that man confers on it, seem to be two ways for spirit to be present (see chapter two above). The spirit present in man shows itself through the medium of his body as an active organizing force leaving its mark on everything it touches. The spirit present in matter, embodied in it in its intelligible content, is, on the contrary, a passive presence, received and borne, simply an effect or vestige of spirit. Man rediscovers these vestiges as the traces of another Spirit who went before him and who, like him, is a dynamic, organizing force, but on another plane. Just as man molds things in his own way, transforming them, giving them a new appearance, a new intelligibility, so also is he obliged to acknowledge that, even before his intervention, these same things already had an appearance proper to them, a prior intelligibility of somewhat the same kind as that which he gives them (which, moreover, is at the bottom of his concept of them). Scientific technique uses knowledge already gathered.

4. Third: This Intelligibility Demands an Explanation

But these traces of spirit in matter cannot simply exist there, without any meaning. The difference between them and the common characteristics of matter (quantitative, sensory, located, measurable, etc.) demands that we seek their origin elsewhere. Just as the specialist in prehistory discovers the presence of man in an archeological excavation by means of the traces of his intelligence (industry, home sites, etc.), so too every logical person must reasonably attribute the traces of spirit in matter to a Spirit who must be their origin. In short, the intelligibility of matter and its relationship with the human spirit demand as an explanation the existence of a Spirit at work within matter.

And this explanation must be of a permanent type. In fact, the intelligibility of matter shows an astonishing stability. All the determinism upon which science is founded is itself an expression of this stability, this structural permanence, which inclines us to think that this supreme source can and must be perennial, never ceasing to exercise its influence.

This point merits reflection because we could be accused of anthropomorphism in transferring what happens in man to what we know about matter. Yet this accusation cannot be levelled against our process of reasoning, which follows the normal line of rational explanation in tracing back a group of facts to a common source. On the contrary, the accusation would be valid if we thought of this source, this supreme Spirit, in the same way as we regard the human spirit. The difference in their effects should warn us of the need to change our point of view. Let's examine the two cases. When man acts upon things to give them a new structure, he always begins with an existing, concrete reality; he uses the first structure of things, their laws and characteristics, to make them express a new idea. Yet his efforts remain outside matter: even splitting the atom did no more than use the forces concealed within it.

If, on the contrary, a Spirit is the source of the intelligibility of matter, his influx can be thought of only as taking place in a radical way; his action must begin in some way "from nothing," [10] and he must not derive his existence from another structure outside that which is created by his activity. This is so because this intelligibility, which is native to matter and for which the Spirit is responsible, is not something extrinsic to matter, something added on to it. It is fundamental, an indelible mark imprinted on matter and reflecting a Spirit who is its cause, a symbol that man can decipher because he, being a spirit, has the key to it.

The consequence of this is important. Since man can shape matter and then put it aside, leaving on it the mark he has placed there, so also the Spirit, having left his imprint on matter, must continue and prolong his influence thereon because of the depth and primal quality of his imprint, which reaches to the very depths of reality.

We have now almost reached the summit of our "way." There the human mind discovers with difficulty, as through a mist, the signs of a Thought, a Spirit, who is the origin of all the intelligibility of things.

We can sum up our approach thus: the material universe, even before human thought acts upon it, contains a basic intelligibility, that is, the germ of the ideas and the laws that the mind will set forth in due course. In the material world there would be an inner relationship to thought, to the mind, even if there were no man to think, to use his mind. And this can be explained logically only by the existence of a Thought who transcends and surpasses both the world of matter and that of the human mind, which are participants in that Thought in two different ways, as we have shown when speaking about the two ways in which spirit can be present in the world.

There are many other "ways" to attain the same result, the same summit, each one beginning from a different experiential basis (the

10 This radical aspect of the divine action is expressed philosophically by the words *ex nihilo.*

contingency of things, causality, etc.); however, all reach the same end from different human perspectives or points of view. They all culminate in the same reality, still vague to the senses, but grasped indirectly at the end of a laborious journey. In somewhat the same way invisible heavenly bodies, emitting Hertzian waves detectable by radio telescopes, tell us very little more than that these bodies exist. Nevertheless, to human reason, the very existence of God reveals itself as penetrating the whole universe and influencing every being profoundly, somewhat as the sun reveals its presence to a blind man by its comforting heat.

III. WHAT CAN WE SAY ABOUT THE "NATURE" OF GOD?

We have already said at the beginning of this chapter that the problem of God is a problem before which human thought must logically acknowledge its limitations. Yet, without lessening the importance of this observation, we can still ask ourselves whether, beginning with the data we have gathered about God's existence, we may not venture some remarks about his nature. Let us take, as it were, the approach of a child who has never known his father, but is aware that his father is alive, and sets out to obtain some information about him from the traces he has left behind.

Obviously, in dealing with the nature of God, we can speak only about an "indirect vision" reaching God only "from outside," because we attain it by deduction from his works. Hence, we shall not forget that his inner life and his interior intensity surpass the capabilities of our thought and can be known only by means of a special divine revelation (by the Faith). We are aware that our knowledge is developed only from sensory, material data, and that our minds can attain intelligible reality only by working on sense data. And we cannot perceive God with our senses but only by his works.

1. God Transcendent and Absolute

As a result of our research we can see that this supreme Spirit has an infinite capacity in the realm of intelligibility since he is the source of the infinitely varied characteristics of things. Man, too, has this quality but only to a limited degree. An engineer shows his genius in his capacity to expand the scope of his works; the wider their application, the richer is his mind in inner resources. How much truer this is of the pure Spirit who affects things, not on the surface, but in the final structures he confers on them!

Hence, we must see this divine Reality as a spiritual and *essentially polyvalent* center of action. It must transcend all particular determinations, because it establishes them all. It must be outside all categories and classifications; it does not belong to any supreme class of being, because it is the source of all being. In a word, it is transcendent.

In the same way, this Spirit must be completely independent of the beings that emanate from him. Basically, these other beings have no absolute existence; the existence that they do possess and that is inscribed in their nature is derived from this unique source. They are only relative beings, dependent upon this Spirit, who alone can therefore be called absolute, the ultimate point of reference, the source of all intelligibility, and hence the foundation of scientific truth. In order to express these characteristics, the name "God" has been reserved exclusively for this Spirit.

2. Unveiling the Face of God

The method of our research, going from the work to the author of the work, allows us to try to say something about him. In fact, because of the causal relationship that exists between God and the intelligible structures of things, these structures must in some way reflect a little of the divine nature just as an author always reveals something of his character, style, etc., in his writings. Yet here, because of the infinite disproportion that exists between Creator and creatures, such an attempt can be made only by taking rigorous precautions as regards method, and it can never result in direct knowledge. We cannot go into detail here about these problems, but we can make some general remarks on the subject.

The intelligibility of created things is shown by a certain number of qualities that seemingly can be attributed analogically to God, qualities that philosophers call "perfections." But we must eliminate from these qualities every imperfection, that is, every reference to the matter in which they are embodied, and then we must raise them to infinity. Of course, "we cannot, without being blasphemous, refuse to attribute to the Creator any of the perfections which creatures possess and of which he is the source. However, his mode of possessing them is not that of creatures. Creatures divide up perfection, whereas God unifies it and erases all limits from it." [11] That is why, in order to avoid attributing to God the created mode of possessing these perfections, St. Thomas thought it better to deny of God the human "manner" in which we express them. That is the meaning of the theory of analogy.

Thus we say that *God is the sum of all the perfections* that exist in the universe but raised to an eminent degree. We must be careful not to understand the term "sum" to mean any juxtaposition of perfections in God. Indeed, by the very fact that each of God's perfections is infinite, they cannot be placed alongside each other because then they would limit each other. In other words, they are intermingled in God, each one expressing the whole divine nature but from a particular human point of view. Man cannot encompass God in the plenitude of his perfection and so he views God by means of concepts that show only partial aspects of the divine nature, aspects that are always tainted with anthropomorphism. In reality, God does not "possess" these perfections; he "is" each one of them and all of them together, but analogically and to an eminent degree in relation to everything we can say about him.[12]

So, since God is a pure spirit, he is not subject to change or modification, that characteristic of matter which is the domain of evolution. Hence God is not in duration or time. There is no development in him; he is "eternal," a word which, however, means nothing to us as regards our experiences, which are always temporal. When speaking of God we must reject temporality; and

---

11 A. Sertillanges, *La philosophie de saint Thomas d'Aquin* Vol. I (Paris, Aubier, 1950), p. 165.

12 This is why we must say that God is known through any one of his perfections, each one being capable of designating him completely. Thus, while we may practice many forms of devotion, we are always striving toward the same end.

we shall not look upon eternity as time without end, but, on the contrary, as the permanence of a present that is always fully rich and that will not pass or be diminished in any way.

On the subject of this divine eternity, we should note that if man is called to live in union with God, it can only be through an exalting participation in this eternity. We can see a faint image of this in the human tendency that is found in intellectual contemplation or in emotional ecstasy, for example, to go beyond time, to be unaware of its passing. Such a participation is far removed from the popular idea of the life to come, seen in human fashion as time without end.

How is God present in the world? Independence from matter seems to us the essential characteristic of all spirit, a characteristic expressing itself in man in the dignity of his person. Clearly, then, God must possess this essential characteristic, the first quality to come to mind when spirituality is being discussed. And this must ultimately mean that God is completely independent of the world.

Therefore, any conception of God as a kind of soul to the world, a great mysterious force identified with nature, is quite inadequate. That would be pantheism, a constant temptation to lower the divine to a natural level, and a more or less romantic tendency. It is the attitude of many scientific minds which are unwilling to embrace radical materialism. They find in pantheism a kind of compromise that will satisfy their vaguely religious sentiments and still avoid the inconveniences of a more precise religious commitment. But this solution is basically irrational. We know how great is the difference between the world of matter and the world of spirit at the level of their mutual relationships in this world. How much more different they must be at the level of pure Spirit?

As we have already seen, though spirit is different from matter, it is still intimately present in it, and this very presence flows from the transcendence of spirit over matter. This is so because God is strangely separate from the world. He is the absolute, the eternal, the fullness of being, supremely self-existing and independent. But if he is all this, everything else outside him, the whole universe, draws its existence, its intelligibility and its duration at every moment from him.

The world is, as it were, suspended from God, who is the most intimate, and also the most different, source of its fluctuating existence. It is precisely because God is the absolute and because the world derives everything from him, that his immanence in the world in no way destroys the infinite difference between him and it. It is because the universe is, as it were, "hitched on to" God, who penetrates it to its very depths, that his presence remains transcendent.

Our imagination often deceives us, making us place God in a localized heaven in outer space; it also misleads us as regards the "solidity" of our universe, concealing from us its precarious nature. We must try to conceive God's presence in the world and his remoteness from it, not thinking of this remoteness in terms of space but in terms of the existence of things and the "solidity" of reality. God is present everywhere anything exists, in the midst of every activity, from the farthest galaxy to the nucleus of the smallest atom; at the same time the infinite polyvalence of his activity reveals the infinite distance that separates him from this world on the level of being.

IV. WHAT IS CREATION?

We can already glimpse what is meant by creation, but here also we must further clarify our ideas. When most believers, and most unbelievers too, think about creation, they have only the concept of a beginning. That, of course, is not a false idea, but it is merely a secondary aspect of a subject which can be known only by faith. Even the lesser importance given to this aspect of the problem may make us forget the essential point upon which theologians, particularly St. Thomas, have insisted, namely, that creation is, above all, a matter of the world's continual dependence on God.

1. What Creation Is Not

Following Father Sertillanges, who contributed so much to the revival of a truer concept of creation, we shall give a summary of certain believers' naive thoughts, which we must avoid. Generally these people think of creation in three stages: first there was nothing; then God created the world; then the world began and continued to exist. This is really a falsification of the divine nature and action.

To say that first there was nothing but God is contradictory. This presupposes a moment when there was really nothing. But in order that a moment should exist, something must exist in it. Our imagination makes us regard time as an empty container ready to receive something, whereas time is only a property of finite reality. If nothing but God exists, then there is no time. Next, these people make the grave mistake of placing God in this nothingness, this empty pseudo-duration. "This would really be atheism because God is suppressed in order to place him in a successive duration which precedes the world and then joins it, and which leaves God open to a wasting away of his being, to change and hence to need." [13] There was no duration in God preceding the world's existence. If we imagine there was, it is only because we cannot form a proper concept of his eternity.

"Then God decided to create." To say this is a further mistake, representing God as first being inactive and then one fine day deciding to create the world. God is not in time and therefore there was no moment in which he created: "No moment can be assigned to the beginning of creation. There is no new deed such as would presuppose a former state, a pre-existence." [14] This would not only place God in time but would postulate a change in him. But he is unchangeable; his creative act is eternal (in the sense of being outside time) and he did not have to do it.

"Finally, the world was created and it existed." That is to say, the divine action was ended, and the whole lamentable popular image was complete, with God contemplating his work from the heights of heaven. (But then what about the inhabitants of the antipodes?) We must admit that while many believers do not harbor such a childish idea, it is often more or less implicit in their beliefs. They view God's action as taking place only at the beginning of the world, or they think of him as being now in an inacces-

---

13 A. Sertillanges, *L'idée de création et ses retentissements en philosophie* (Paris, Aubier, 1945), p. 10.
14 Sertillanges, *op. cit.*, p. 14.

sible heaven. Either way, he is purely and simply left out of things. If God means very little to many people today, it is partly because of these childish notions. Here perhaps more than anywhere else, the faith of many Christians has not gone beyond the stage of the religious instruction they received as children, when these simplified representations were conceivable. Here too the time lag mentioned in our first chapter is plain to see. The adult believer feels an acute need to make a widely developed worldly culture fit in with a religious faith that has not grown at the same rate, and Marxism can easily exploit this discrepancy as a sign of the death of religion. We believe that this is one of the places where a believing scientist must bring his greatest effort to bear, in order to rediscover a truer concept of the nature of God and his relationship with the world and mankind.

2. What Creation Is

We can now better understand what creation really is. It is above all the relationship of dependence that exists between the creature and its Creator. All things, man included, are as it were "suspended" from God, who acts in their inmost recesses, as the source of their being and their activity. The consequences of this doctrine are immense. God is present at the heart of this world and in our own hearts, a fact in which the life of religion finds immediate nourishment because we do not have to leave aside the duties of our state in life or our normal occupations in order to find God. In the next chapter we shall consider another type of divine presence which will reinforce and clarify the one we have just mentioned.

In order to better understand this idea of dependence we must isolate it from the concept of beginning, at least momentarily. Only faith teaches us that the existence of the world had a beginning, that it does not reach back into limitless time. St. Thomas thought that the hypothesis of an ever-existing world (in which Aristotle believed), and hence a world that is eternal in the sense of being without temporal limits, does not conflict with a true idea of creation. Since creation means principally a relationship of dependence, then to extend it to infinity, far from destroying it, grants it its total meaning. An eternal world would need God perhaps even more than a world that had a beginning. For example, on an electric railway the overhead electric cable is supported by a wire that keeps it horizontal; the existence of this wire would be just as indispensable if the railroad were infinite in length.

On this point, we must remark how a return to the traditional concept of creation makes pointless the famous arguments of the last century between materialists and spiritualists about the possible eternity of the world. Both parties bound up the existence of God with the beginning of the world, the materialists to deny his existence, the spiritualists to defend it. The fact that the world did have a beginning is a truth of the Faith properly so called and cannot be proved by arguments from reason; we can prove only that it does not contradict scientific data. It follows from what we have said above that science can never disprove that all things had an absolute beginning because such a beginning is inaccessible to science. For science deals only with that which is measurable, and an absolute beginning cannot be pinpointed because to pinpoint something it must be fixed in relation to something else. Nothingness cannot be a point of reference.

V. GOD'S ACTION IN THE WORLD

The importance of the proper concept of creation is immense because every activity, in the heart of the world and of man, has God as its origin and as the source of its intelligibility. Thus our approach to the world of matter and our contact with it, far from turning us away from God, should on the contrary be a perpetual opportunity for encountering him. Our contact with other men is also a great occasion for meeting God; however, since this area of activity has been made the object of a special divine intervention (charity), we shall speak about it in the next chapter.

How are we to regard this divine action in the universe without yielding to the perpetual temptation to think of God as acting in the same way as men do? We must think of it on a symbolic, truly divine level, which we shall now try to describe more exactly.

The nature of God's presence in the world has led us to think of it as a fundamental influence which maintains each individual thing in its own proper nature. Each thing's nature makes it what it is and, at the same time, is the source of its specific action.

Let us take an example which, though oversimplified, is still enlightening. Electricity has many uses, and can produce different, even opposite, effects—cold in a refrigerator, heat in a heater. It gives light and causes a great variety of movements in different apparatuses, from the electric locomotive to the electric razor. It is always the same force at work in different ways, yet it cannot be seen in its pure state but only in its effects (magnetic, chemical, heat-producing), and these tell us whether the current is flowing or not.

Now, if someone who was completely ignorant of the existence of electricity saw the wide range of electrical appliances, he would never suspect that the same force could produce cold and heat, for example. Only the existence of a conductor and the fact that the current could be cut off would show him the existence of a polyvalent source of power for all the appliances. Carrying the comparison still further, we see that in any one of the appliances, the sheer reality of the effect (the production or non-production of the effect) is entirely attributable to electricity, while the specific effect itself (i.e., cold, heat or light) is entirely attributable to the structure of the appliance in question. Hence I can say, for example, that the ice cubes that I take from my refrigerator are completely produced by electricity or by the appliance, according as I refer to the existence of the product or to the specific function of the apparatus.

We can apply this comparison to God's action with the necessary qualifications. The divine action, far from injuring or even paralleling the action of creatures, constitutes that action in its proper order, penetrates it deeply, keeps it in existence, but leaves it its power of specification. Yet, unlike our example of electricity, since there is no conductor here, and since the divine "current" cannot be switched off, the human mind, so easily beclouded by material objects, does not spontaneously see the presence of God's essentially polyvalent activity, which explains all other activities and is the basis of their dignity. Furthermore—and this is an important difference between the two examples—electrical appliances need electricity only to run them and do not depend on it for their very existence; whereas God is not only the source of creatures' activities but he is also the source of their innate structures (their intelligibility) and their existence.

Therefore, in every created activity, at the heart of the universe, we can say that every effect is both entirely attributable to God on the plane of existence (i.e., the fact that it is a reality) and is also entirely attributable to the creature on the plane of specification (that it is this or that particular thing). The divine action cannot be confused with the creature's action since it is not on the same plane. God's action is not scientifically detectable because science deals only with the specific, observable structures of things. Yet reason can discover God's action by the creature's inability to explain its own intelligibility, as we have seen above.

Therefore, the scientist is certain that in playing his role fully as a scientist he will never be in danger of contradicting the Faith, because everything that he will discover, far from being an obstacle to his encounter with God, will instead be for him a vestige, a mark, of the divine thought always at work in the world. Hence, even if he succeeds in synthesizing life, or explaining evolution, these things will be only a part of the face of God that he will see incarnated in his work.

God's action in the world does not "short-circuit" that of creatures, but penetrates them to establish their originality. It is called first causality in relation to the action of creatures, which is called secondary causality. We can thus see how a doctrine such as evolution has seemed to many people a more religious approach than any other—God working in the living universe by means of an inner urging, as the source of the differentiation of species; not as a *deus ex machina* present locally behind each phenomenon to give each an immediate explanation, perhaps concurring with the explanation sought by science.

There are many other aspects of this doctrine of providence governing the world. One in particular is the idea that all activities are governed, are given a foreseen end, an orientation. And that is an important part of our problem. Where is the world going? What aim did God have in creating it, in preserving it in existence, in giving it its structures, in making it progress through cosmic and biological evolution? Obviously, the answer to these questions is of capital importance and it should be already discernible in what we have said so far. But why confine ourselves to the faint indications we have found when God has taken care to make his divine plan clear and explicit in a direct revelation, his Son? We shall examine this revelation in the next chapter, where we shall approach it in the proper light and with the right key to its meaning.

VI. CONCLUSION

Now, at the end of this investigation, we can take the true measure of the world's relationship to God. The world is God's continual work, emanating from him not as a part of his Being but as a reflection of his thought and his omnipotence. From this we can learn two things. First, since God is the source of the intelligibility of things, it is only in him that they take on their full, true meaning, their whole significance. It is true that by contemplating each creature, isolated from the rest, an undemanding mind can gain an immediate satisfaction. But let one rise a little above the multiplicity of forms in an attempt to obtain a wider vision. It is only by placing the whole panorama in the perspective of a creative Thought that one can give it harmony and coherence, in somewhat the same way as the design in some flowerbeds can be seen only from a height. To take another example, a carpet can be viewed from the upper or the under side. In either case it is the same carpet and the threads are the same, but from the underside it seems strange and disordered because the design on the upper side cannot be seen.

This need for God as the light of the world is confirmed by the testimony of sincere atheists who declare that the world is absurd: for example, Rostand (see his "immense bric-a-brac of nature") or Camus (*The Rebel*). When we reflect on them, these reactions are enlightening. Saying that the world is absurd, that it has no meaning, basically makes an implicit reference to a possible meaning for the world; it expresses a disappointment and witnesses to an unavowed nostalgia for a world that would have meaning. And

what does "have a meaning" signify? It means to have an explanation, an intelligibility that does not reside in the heart of the world
considered in itself (for in this case, it has been declared absurd),
but that must exist somewhere. Without that meaning one should
not make any judgment about the world; it is as it appears and
nothing more. Rostand and Camus were right; in itself the world is
absurd, a thing without meaning. We can also conclude that all
man's efforts at penetrating and dominating this universe have only
one possible justification, that of finding a meaning in the world,
aside from its parts, a meaning in a Thought and an Absolute that
has left his mark on it.

From the opposite point of view, if God alone explains the
world, the world shows us God, as the sun's reflection shows us the
sun. This is a true divine revelation, a primordial revelation, a
background for the other revelation, total and explicit, that of
Christ. Far from destroying or lessening the value of the first, this
revelation of Christ throws it into greater relief and gives it a
greater usefulness.

The renewal of biblical studies has made clear that this discovery of God in his work was one of the major lessons of the bible.
Indeed the Church has made it one of her dogmas.[15] The Fathers
of the Church developed this theme with an enthusiasm that the
modern world has rather forgotten since the coming of Jan-
senism.[16] Christian spirituality has made it food for meditation to
such an extent that for St. Francis, for example, to love God's
handiwork was to love God himself.

Therefore, when modern man is tempted to separate his contact
with the world from his religious life, he should rejoin this great
tradition according to which, as Claudel writes: "There is not a

---

[15] See E. Beaucamp, *The Bible and the Universe* (Westminster, Md., The
Newman Press, 1963), and *Lumière et Vie*, No. 14, 1954. This teaching
is found especially in the Psalms (e.g., Pss. 19 and 104), and in St. Paul
(Rom. 1, 20). Vatican Council I (1870) defined the doctrine: "The same
Holy Mother Church holds and teaches that God, the beginning and end
of all things, can be known with certitude by the natural light of human
reason from created things" (Third Session, Chapter 2, *On Revelation*).

[16] There are numerous texts from the Fathers on this subject in the
important book by C. Tresmontant, *Christian Metaphysics* (New York,
Sheed & Ward, 1965).

religious universe and a profane universe: there is only one single revelation handed down in an ineffable . . . language." [17]

Hence, for the believing scientist, it is a truly Christian way of encountering the God of Abraham, the same God who reveals himself in his work in the world as well as in the history of Israel and in his Son. God's revelation of himself in his Son is the last stage of our investigation and the one upon which we shall now embark.

[17] P. Claudel, *Présence et prophétie*, (Fribourg, Libr. univers., 1942), p. 273.

V
MEETING GOD
IN CHRIST

In the preceding pages, we have seen that the world began from God in a sort of descending movement. We have seen some rays of light that partially show the brightness of their source. All creatures, including man himself, are works that continually pour forth from the one transcendent source, God the Creator.

But that is not all. A closer look at the heart of the world reveals that all the beings that comprise it, whether living or not, are subject to continual mutations, changes, and renewals. Nothing about them is fixed. Modern science, desirous of finding a possible meaning for this apparently disordered jumble, has systematized this elementary mass by means of concepts such as cosmogenesis and evolution.

What meaning can these mutations and changes have in the purely religious sphere, the sphere of the relationship of all beings with their source, God the Creator? From its very beginning, Christianity was struck by this evolution. Not only did it see in things the springing forth of an omnipotent divine power in a descending movement; it also saw things as animated by a vast ascending movement expressed by the idea of a return to God and essentially realized by the intervention of Christ calling man to play a major role in that return. That is the subject of this chapter.

I. THE RETURN OF CREATURES TO GOD

1. Creatures Accomplish This Return by Their Special Characteristics

How can we form a more precise idea of the return of all things to God? Logically it should be like this. Since all creatures, in their different orders, make real a divine idea, a creative project, they return to God by carrying out his plans and by unfolding their own perfections. God's works are not inert. It is in exercising their dynamism that they accomplish this ascent and render glory to their author. "For God calls all things to existence, to life, to activity, not from without, but from within; not by uttering a word, but by forming things, endowing them with a structure and an orientation. . . . He calls to the birds to spread their wings to the wind, to soar and to sing, each with a note of its own, from the humble chirping of the sparrow to the pure, liquid plaint of the nightingale. Every creature answers the call. They yield to the vital impulse that sweeps them along, they give free way to their own abounding energies, and, in this happy obedience, the thing they seek is their own fulfillment and their own perfection: for the water, it is to flow; for the rose, to bloom; for the bird, to sing its song. More deeply still, it is an image of God they seek in this fruition of their being; it is God himself whom they seek and find without knowing it." [1] Therefore, it is this unconscious aspiration, this basic tendency to expand, to accomplish that for which they are made, that explains the return of all creatures to their author, manifesting his thought in infinitely varied ways.

One of the merits of science is precisely that it has discovered in concrete fashion, on the plane of determinism, the meaning of this tendency—the ascent of beings in evolution. This tendency is toward an ever more complex organization, an ever more complete independence of material surroundings, culminating in the appearance of man, who is himself caught up in a progress that prolongs this urge which he takes in hand.[2]

These two movements are expressed in the ancient formula: God is the Alpha and Omega of all things. The whole universe comes from him and, in its whole structure, is made to return to him by obeying the laws that rule it. The scientist who discovers or uses these laws is simply taking advantage of this mysterious

---

[1] J. Mouroux, *The Meaning of Man* (New York, Doubleday, 1961), p. 33; quoted by permission of the publisher.

[2] The doctrine of evolution has developed, especially in the last century, outside of, and even in opposition to, the religious preoccupations of Christians routinely limited to a fixed concept of creation and unable to see in evolution its convergence with the traditional doctrine of the dynamic return of creatures to God.

ascent, this glorification of God that every creature whispers, inviting him to join it. If he accepts the invitation, he will find God in the very heart of his work. We can speak about the finality of the universe because it is the only finality that is truly certain and that eludes all scientific criticism since, by definition, it is brought about by the determinism of nature.[3]

2. Man's Place in This Return

(a) Domination of the Universe

One of the most enlightening facts of science in this area is the restoration of man to his position at the heart of the cosmos. We see him intimately bound up with this world by his membership in the animal kingdom (for St. Thomas, metaphysically speaking, man belongs to the animal genus). We also see him as emerging from this world by reason of his superior psychological life, as the scientist would say, or because of his spiritual soul, according to the philosopher. His role then seems to be to complete creation since, by a kind of divine delegation, he has been made head and master of the universe that he must dominate.

In fact, since he appeared on the scene, man has shown a tendency to dominate nature from which he came and to master it with his thought. Today this tendency has surged forward by the spread of the human species all over the world and especially by the extraordinary mastery of science and technology over nature in true fulfillment of the commandment given by God to the first man.[4]

Yet the domination of the universe is only a bare fact. To dominate implies an orientation, a use of this mastery. What meaning should it have? Obviously, it means that man has a place in the great ascent of all things to God so that he may facilitate it. Man's mastery over nature has meaning only if it enters this current to help it and even to accelerate it. How can this be? By his attaining that which he himself has been made for.

[3] See above, chapter three.
[4] Gen. 1, 28: "Then God blessed them and said to them, 'Be fruitful and multiply; fill the earth and subdue it. Have dominion over the fish of the sea, the birds of the air, the cattle and all the animals. . .' "

Man is a creature, too. He is part of the cosmos that must return to God. But each creature partakes in this return by attaining its proper perfection (its structure, the divine idea in it). And what is man's perfection but the fulfillment of his being, the primacy of spiritual values and the establishment of a free, rational order?

Man's role in this ascending movement is of the first importance. By his consciousness, his enlightenment, and his love, he must participate in it in order to better express the testimony of the other creatures whom he has been called to dominate. He is, as it were, the priest of creation; on the natural level, he is a sort of conscious mediator between things and their Creator. In the last part of this chapter we shall see how, in union with Christ, man must play this part in a very concrete way, by his work. Here we shall speak only in general about this idea.

(b) Human Destiny

Still, before playing this role, and in order not to betray it, man must recognize the fact that he should first take his place in this ascent to God by attaining his own perfection, that is, by fulfilling his proper destiny.

We have already acknowledged that human perfection is realized in man in an original way—in freedom: in the infinite expansion of his spiritual horizon which leads him to tend toward an ideal of happiness and development by means of his desires. Attaining his desires in ephemeral, imperfect things does not give him satisfaction or lasting joy. Again, many psychologists (as well as the existentialists) have noted that one of man's characteristics is his special power to be sad and anxious. This is an indication that the human heart is made for something other than mere earthly satisfactions. Man's spiritual thought exposes him unconsciously to infinite perspectives and urges him to look everywhere for the absolute, the definitive, the impeccable.[5]

In short, in all his actions, man shows this inborn tendency that urges him ceaselessly to look further, to progress toward some unique and necessary absolute. Teilhard de Chardin has described this basic urge that distinguishes man and isolates him from the rest of the animal world.

[5] Daily life offers endless examples of this search for the definitive, the impeccable: from the collector always seeking for the matchless work of art to the Don Juan who is never satisfied with his conquests.

This call of the infinite, resounding across and by means of all the beings that surround and entice man, finds its great explanation in the general framework of the return to God. This is so because, having been created by God, man can find his true development, his complete joy, only by living in union with his Creator, in ascending toward him, in giving him glory by knowledge and love. If we remember that man has been made for God this strange longing is explained. Created by God, obviously he can find his joy only in him, in doing that for which he was made.

But there is a danger that we may stop at this purely mental stage; that would empty it of all meaning. Hitler often ended his speeches with a reference to God, but that did not civilize his actions since his reference was confined to a purely conceptual or emotional level. For man, a reference to God is above all a work to be done, a wish to be carried out.[6]

Let us examine this thought more closely. God, the Absolute Being, is not known directly by human knowledge, because, of itself, it deals directly with sensory reality alone, knowing spiritual things only indirectly through sensible things. God is a hidden God, and it is both the tragedy and the greatness of man's condition that he is made to develop in the knowledge and love of God, who nevertheless remains hidden from him.

That is why some divine revelations (apart from the supernatural revelation in Christ) is of itself indispensable for human existence. Thus, at this purely natural level, God reveals himself to man and becomes indirectly accessible to him through the medium of his works that make up creation. As we saw at the end of the last chapter, by the very fact that all creatures are signs of God, his manifestations, his natural revelations, fundamentally man must build his development upon them by giving glory to the Creator as seen through his created traces. That is the basic divine plan whose broad outlines and demands remain, despite the historical vicissitudes introduced by sin; even sin will be integrated as a principal element in Christ's plan.

Thus God, the transforming goal of human life, the pole attracting that cosmic progress which man must help to build, reveals

---

[6] See our Lord's warning: "Not everyone who says to me, 'Lord, Lord,' shall enter the kingdom of heaven, but he who does the will of my Father in heaven shall enter the kingdom of heaven." (Mt. 7, 21).

himself in a primordial way in his creation. From the fact that creatures have God as their author and that they unconsciously tend toward him, they carry in themselves, in a certain way and to some degree, a more or less distant resemblance to him. These traces of God can reveal him to every lucid mind. The mind can discover, under their material appearances, the presence of the Being for which that mind has been made. It must be aware of the essential indigence of these traces, their precariousness, their inability to explain themselves and the message they contain.

Since man himself is the most perfect material creature, a spirit embodied in matter (he is not a mere trace but a likeness of God), he should be able to manifest more clearly than all other creatures this message and natural revelation. Human relations should be the best occasions for a meeting with God.[7] The signs of man's participation in the general return to God are thus very clear—seeking God through the fulfillment of his own human nature (the natural law) by means of creatures, using them in conformity with the divine plan for them.

3. The Great Obstacle to This Return—Sin

But why must man have such difficulty in discovering God in his works? That is a mystery that defies our logic; it is an inexplicable fact. For a long time psychologists have been studying the possibility that man will suffer a reverse in the pursuit of his destiny. While other beings in the world attain (unconsciously, it is true) the end for which they were made, spontaneously finding their way, man gives the impression that he is afflicted with a congenital weakness, whence comes his sadness, his disquiet, and his dissatisfaction. Normally, in the logical course of events, he should fulfill God's plan with ease, finding God spontaneously in the traces he has left everywhere, especially in human love.

But in fact we are obliged to acknowledge that the reality is far different. Man, instead of going to God, stops at creatures and obviously does not find the joy for which he was made. In desiring and pursuing created things, he tries to quench in them his thirst

---

[7] This is the natural basis upon which Christian charity will build.

for the infinite and the absolute, and the disappointment he experiences when he possesses them, far from teaching him a lesson, urges him on to new pursuits and new illusions.

In doing this, man is somewhat like a child on the seashore at night. The moon, veiled in clouds, glitters on the waves far out to sea, and the child is enchanted with what he sees. Unaware of the source of the shining reflections, he is attracted to them and, thinking they are real, runs into the sea to gather them up; but all he finds is cold water slipping through his fingers. That is what man does. He has within him an invincible tendency toward, and yearning for, the absolute, the definitive, the perfect; and when he sees traces of these qualities in creatures, he desires the creatures passionately, because he believes that what he sees in them is real— whereas it is only a reflection of something else. He does everything to possess them, and when he does, they not only do not bring him joy but leave him with a feeling of emptiness that increases with each new attempt to fill it.

If man takes the trouble to reflect, he will be able to see how illogical his conduct is. This disappointment and disillusionment, so deeply rooted in the human heart, can be explained only by a lamentable blindness, a failure to see that all the charms and attractions of creatures have no real existence in themselves. They are only traces, reflections of an absolute reality, God. It is only normal that man should reach out toward these reflections, because he is made for their source, God; but it is not normal for him to stop there.

Stopping at creatures constitutes evil for man. That is, it is a cessation of his ascent to God; it is what we call "sin." From a legalistic point of view, sin is defined as an infraction of God's law. Following God's law simply means doing the things for which man was made. Again, sin should be recognized as the great weakness preventing man from finding the fullness of joy, turning him away from his true destiny, and making him treat some creature, especially himself (pride), as an absolute. The creature then loses its "transparence." Darkened by sin, it no longer allows man to see God through it; it becomes opaque to his eyes and acquires an illusory solidity, in somewhat the same way as a jet of water, flowing compactly and silently from a fountain, seems so solid that we forget for a moment that it is a liquid and must be fed from some source. So it is that the solidity of creatures and their charms make us forget that they flow from, and continually depend on, God.[8]

We must remark, however, that, while sin is a great disruption of the order willed by God, it does not itself reside in the created object. The very enchantment and pleasure it promises are but the reflections and the prediction of the divine reality. The evil resides essentially in the human soul that refuses to accept the order of things, turns the creature away from its original purpose in order to monopolize it, and forgets that the attraction which the creature exercises is only the echo of an attraction of another kind.

A scientist must not forget that he runs a certain risk, which is also his greatest temptation. Working on the very heart of material things, he risks being carried away by the excitement of research and forgetting the profound meaning of his activity. There is danger for him in mastering the material world; yet this is his proper mission because mastery of the universe, far from resulting in man's monopolizing creatures for his own use, should be essentially a kind of stewardship for another purpose—helping in the great cosmic ascent toward God.[9]

[8] Hence, sin is either a blindness of the mind, a weakness of the will, or both together. The Faith explains our propensity to sin by the dogma of original sin, which left man with this permanent weakness, this tendency to stop at creatures and so to retard his ascent to God. There are two principles in man (matter and spirit), and sin plays on this dichotomy, amplifying it and posing a threat to a balance that is always unstable at best. The struggle against sin should therefore start with a restoration of rational order in man, not smothering completely the lower tendencies, which are good in themselves, but simply ruling them by reason.

[9] Because sin is the great disturbance of the order of things willed by God, a life of sin can only result in disgust and disillusionment. When the creature is cut off from its divine source and end, it is incapable of bringing true joy and happiness to the human heart. This is also why the basic way of finding God is the renunciation of creatures—the goods of this world, human love, and especially one's own will—considered not as evil but as occasions of sin. This is the way chosen by religious (in Orders, Congregations or Institutes). The other way, followed by those "in the world," tries to find God's plan, to ascend toward him through creatures, with the risk of stopping at them. Hence this way to God requires continual vigilance ("Watch and pray!"). The two ways of religious perfection are based on the supernatural help given by Christ: namely, grace.

II. CHRIST, THE PRINCIPAL AGENT IN THE RETURN TO GOD

We can now more easily understand why God, in his love, has revealed himself in a fuller and more definitive way. Since his self-revelation in creatures was full of ambiguity because of sin, which made it difficult to use creatures properly, he willed to show himself in a more visible fashion in his Son, thus putting himself more within our reach. In this way, he also gave to the world a new energy, a divine dynamism, capable of making man's efforts effective in bringing about the cosmic return to God. Finally, God thus opened up to man the exalted perspective of a destiny that culminates in God, whom man can now reach, not merely from outside, but by sharing in God's own life.[10]

Thus Christ, the Son of God made man, appears as the efficacious agent of the great ascent of creatures toward God, through human effort. But we must first define what the title "Son of God" means, because therein lies the basis of Christ's mission; and we cannot do this without saying something about the Trinity, the source of all this dynamism and the object of man's destiny.

1. Christ and the Trinity

The Trinity, the inner life of God, is called a mystery, not because it is unintelligible in itself, but because our minds, due to their limitations, are unable to understand God.[11] Nevertheless, theology, which is a rational attempt to understand the truths of the Faith, can give us certain insights.

How can we describe the Trinity, the inner life of God, in which Christ invites us to share? The simplest way is to have recourse to a simile, because the bible tells us that man is created in the image of God and so he must be like his Creator in some way. Indeed, every artist or engineer leaves in his work, particularly in a work that he regards as his most beautiful, something of his main concern, his manner of thinking, his character, his inner nature.

---

[10] Theologians discuss whether the motive for the incarnation was solely the destruction of sin (the redemption) or whether it was part of God's original plan. In any event, at his creation man was raised to the supernatural state (participation in the divine life) which he later lost by original sin.

[11] See above, chapter one, for our remarks on the subject of mysteries.

Man is an image of God, not by reason of his body, which he has in common with the animals, but by reason of his soul, which is his own special characteristic. Now what does his soul do when it is in action? By his intelligence, man knows what things are, a knowledge which is expressed in ideas that are the products of his mind, concepts by means of which he represents reality to himself.[12] If an idea is in conformity with the thing known and if it corresponds to a need, the human mind will desire this thing and will love it because of the idea it has formed of it. That is why, if the idea does not correspond with reality, love begets disillusionment. Hence, in man there is a trilogy: the mind that knows, the idea that it forms and by means of which it knows, and the love that flows from these two elements.

This trilogy should be found also in God, due allowance being made for the infinite difference between man and his Creator. God does not know as we do. We know things outside ourselves, independent of us and autonomous in themselves. But God is at every instant the cause of everything that exists; he knows things by the very fact that he causes them to exist. We can say that he knows them from within, as the artist knows his work to the degree that it is the fruit of his activity. Hence, we can say that when God knows a being other than himself, he knows it in the depths of his own Being. In short, we can say that the object of God's knowledge is God himself.

Having made this twofold allowance, how can we discover in God the trilogy that we found in the human soul? God, insofar as he is a spirit, the source of every other activity in him, is the Father, the first Person of the Trinity.

God knows himself, a knowledge that is expressed in an idea that he has of himself, a mental, inner word, as the philosophers say ("word" is *logos* in Greek, *verbum* in Latin). This idea that God has of himself, begotten by him from all eternity, is the Son, the Word of God, the second Person of the Trinity.

Finally, God loves himself in his Word. Hence, this love of God for himself is begotten of the first two Persons: he is the Holy Spirit, the third Person of the Trinity.

We should note that all this is only an analogical explanation in human terms. In God, these realities that we have discovered are

[12] See chapter two above on the development of ideas.

subsisting Persons, yet they do not multiply the divine nature, for God remains one.

The Faith rightly insists on this idea of Persons in God. If we recall what we said about the human person we can glimpse a little of the meaning of the mystery of the Trinity. Personality implies autonomy, or absolute independence, and the inner richness proper to a spiritual being. In itself, the spirit is seen as a center of activity, the great source of intelligibility and, at the same time, a power for unification. Hence, a true communion between two beings is always of a spiritual nature. Even two material things are said to be alike because they share in one and the same idea embodied in both, matter alone preventing a closer union between them; and if there is a real union, such as a chemical combination or a biological assimilation, the two elements lose their original nature, or at least one of them does.

On the contrary, two human beings can be united by knowledge and especially by love (having the same tastes, ideas, etc.). Here the communion is deeper, the identification more profound, and it does not destroy the richness of either. But here, too, matter (the body) is an obstacle. The gestures of human love are vain attempts to overcome the obstacle, and kissing or embracing leaves the lovers still in their personal solitude.

Thus we conclude that in God, who is a pure spirit, the life of the Trinity consists in an intimate communion, an exchange of the highest degree of richness, between the divine Persons, the sources of the relations in the Trinity. Hence, the life of the Trinity does not depend upon its external activity, creation, which is only the radiation of a richness that is sufficient unto itself. We shall deal with this point later. Now let us see where Christ's mission fits into this doctrine.

2. Christ's Human Mission

Why did the second Person of the Trinity become man? This second revelation should extend and transcend the first because creatures, by the very fact that they are more or less images of God, correspond to divine ideas or plans, as we may say in human terms. But, as we have seen, God has only one idea of himself, namely, his Son, the Word of God. And so, "just as the artist works according to an idea conceived in his mind, so too God has produced creatures by his Word, who is his Son" (St. Thomas). These two revelations of God therefore follow the same line—after the created works of God, which are reflections of him, comes the very Idea of God, the divine Word, the model for every divine work.

Since the revelation of God in his creatures is inoperative; and since evil and sin make the use of creatures perilous and difficult; and since, nevertheless, God is more than ever the only true aim of human life, the only source of happiness and joy; we can easily understand why he willed to make another revelation, the most meaningful one possible for us—becoming one among us in his Son.

Thus the Second Person of the Trinity, the Word of God, became man in the historical Christ. This revelation of God, of necessity the last, the only complete and total one, is henceforth the only effective means for every man to find, know, and love God. Therefore, this mission of Christ's is not only a redemption of sinful humanity; it also opens up a new life for man.

In fact, Christ came not only to destroy the disorder introduced by sin, the break between God and man, and to offer every man the possibility (by his resurrection) of overcoming the temptation to make an illusory god of a creature; but, because he united divinity and humanity in his Person, he also raised humanity to a height to which it could never have aspired, one which transcends the relationship of creature to Creator. In a word, he has given every man the chance to become an adopted son of God. By sharing in our human nature, he, the true Son of God, has enabled all men to have access to God's own life, to the riches of the life of the Trinity. He has called them to enjoy the immeasurable happiness of God Himself.[13]

---

[13] This supernatural raising of human nature is accomplished by a divine aid, sanctifying grace, a kind of second nature. It is the source of activities that are performed at the level of the divine life and that are normally fed by means of love of God and the sacraments.

3. Christ's Cosmic Mission

The classical expositions of this doctrine are generally limited to its purely human side. Even when they do touch on certain communal aspects of Christ's work, they are frequently silent about its cosmic repercussions. But the renewed interest in the bible and in the Fathers of the Church has restored to a place of honor this important, traditional part of the Christian Faith. Since it touches closely upon the problem that concerns us here, namely the combination of the Christian life and the life of science, we must pause to consider it. It is of the utmost importance "to emphasize that Christ came not only for the redemption of souls, nor for the liberation of humanity, but for the salvation of the entire world. The Christian message means little in certain quarters given up to technology and science. This is because the real message has been unconsciously mutilated and emasculated till it appears totally irrelevant to the lives of those who are absorbed in their effort to dominate nature." [14]

The general idea of this cosmic role of Christ flows from God's great plan for the universe and man. Since all beings, having come from God, should return to him by bearing witness to his greatness and love, and since man ought to play a primary part in this return, Christ, who is both God and man, reveals himself as the great architect of this return, this glorification of God.

As the *Logos,* the Word of God, Christ is intimately bound up with creation, as we have seen before. This is the fundamental theme with which St. John began his gospel: "In the beginning was the Word, and the Word was with God; and the Word was God. . . . All things were made through him, and without him was made nothing that has been made" (Jn. 1, 1. 3), a teaching that is also found in St. Paul: "For in him were created all things in the heavens and on the earth, things visible and things invisible" (Col. 1, 16).

The action of the *Logos* is not confined to the act of creation.

---

[14] P. Beaucamp, *The Bible and the Universe* (Westminster, Md., The Newman Press, 1963), p. 174. This book shows clearly the biblical foundation for Christ's cosmic work, and we recommend it highly. See also S. Lyonnet, "La Rédemption de l'univers" in *Lumière et Vie,* No. 48, 1960, p. 43-62.

By his becoming man, he afforded a really effective power for accomplishing God's great plan: "He was in the world, and the world was made through him, and the world knew him not. He came unto his own, and his own received him not. But to as many as received him he gave the power of becoming sons of God" (Jn. 1, 10-12).

Tradition has often linked this passage with a text from the prophet Isaiah which is very explicit on the double movement, descending and ascending, of the divine action: "For just as from the heavens, the rain and snow come down and do not return there till they have watered the earth, making it fertile and fruitful, giving seed to him who sows and bread to him who eats, so shall my word be that goes forth from my mouth; it shall not return to me void, but shall do my will, achieving the end for which I sent it" (Is. 55, 10-11).

By his incarnation and redemption, the Word of God fulfilled this plan of fructification that goes beyond the framework of the strictly human. Indeed, the bible does not regard man as isolated from the world. In sacred scripture, man's immersion in the world is a commonplace truth. Nature, too, has been affected by sin and shares in the lot of man, its master.[15] Consequently, when Christ redeemed man, he also redeemed the world. He did it by means of his human body, which is a part of the world and destined to be transfigured. But St. Paul goes further and speaks of a true redemption of the world; each time he mentions Christ's mission, he extends it from man to the entire cosmos. It has been said that, according to St. Paul, "if we could see the whole universe simultaneously, past, present and future, we would see that every being depends ontologically upon Christ and is intelligible only through him." [16]

In his Epistle to the Romans, St. Paul describes in expressive terms the whole of creation waiting for redemption: "For we know that all creation groans and travails in pain until now. And not only it, but we ourselves also who have the first-fruits of the Spirit —we ourselves groan within ourselves, waiting for the adoption as

[15] See, among other texts, Gen. 3, 17-18; and Gen. 4, 12: "When thou shalt till [the soil], it shall not yield to thee its fruit."

[16] J. Huby, *Saint Paul; les épîtres de la captivité* (Paris, Beauchesne, 1937), p. 40.

sons, the redemption of our body" (Rom. 8, 22-23). This is a basic Christian theme, too often forgotten in the individualism of the last few centuries. St. Peter, too, spoke of "the restoration of all things" by Christ (Acts 3, 21), while St. John in his Apocalypse looked forward to "a new heaven and a new earth" (Apoc. 21, 1).

Thus the whole universe shares in the destiny of the human nature taken on by the Son of God. As St. Thomas says: "Since all material things exist in some fashion for man's sake, it is fitting that the state of the whole material universe shall then undergo a transformation so that it may be adapted to the state of man." [17]

For, in the last analysis, man is the essential beneficiary of Christ's work. Nor must we forget that the aim of that work is man's sharing in the life of the Trinity. Of course, God does not need man or the cosmos; he need not have created them. The creation, an operation *ad extra* as the theologians call it, was not indispensable to God's life but is only a radiation of it. If we remember that the life of the Trinity is above all a vital communion between the three Persons, we shall understand that God's object in creating the universe and man, its crowning glory, was to associate other persons, other beings, images of God, with this same community of the Trinity. The human person has, then, an immeasurable dignity, that of being called to share in such a destiny. The scientist must never forget this fact, and his work upon the structure of the cosmos must always be motivated by it.

It is therefore easy to understand how deeply this doctrine is embedded in the very heart of our philosophy: *this universe redeemed by Christ is the material upon which the scientist works;* hence, he is called to cooperate in transforming it, as we shall see. The essential thing now is to see the importance of this theme. In too many books about the faith of the scientist, this religious attitude is limited to discovering the meaning of the creation, that is, the descending movement in the divine plan, with the result that the scientist is invited only to encounter a vague "God of philosophers and scientists." But to stop there would be to cut the ascending movement out of the divine plan and to forget that Christ cannot be separated from it. Like all men, the scientist is called, not only to adore, but also to work and cooperate in transforming the whole universe in Christ; and, by doing this, he accomplishes a

17 *Summa contra gentiles,* IV. 97.

mission that only he can fulfill because of his daily contact with matter.

Thus, the union between the life of the scientist and that of the believer does not take place on a merely natural level but is brought about at the very heart of Christianity because of its most basic demands.

III. THE SCIENTIST'S CHRISTIAN VOCATION

This brings us to the conclusion of our search. All that we have said so far allows us now to place the scientist's vocation more precisely in a Christian setting. And since the scientist's work is only one form of human labor, we must simply specify what a theology of work implies when applied to this particular area, science.

1. Science Spiritualizes Matter

What place does scientific work have in the divine plan for the return of all things to God? Many people will reply that the religious purpose of such work is to expiate sin. Because of the effort that research demands, it can be a source of merit and a means of sanctification. This is true but it limits the perspective to a purely negative and rather pessimistic horizon because progress in eliminating the arduous part of research (manual labor) would inevitably result in taking away the religious value attached to this human effort.

The true answer is quite different and should be part of a larger vision. We could say that science, by its discoveries, continues the work of creation and prolongs its influence. That is better than the first answer but it would be limited to the descending movement of God's plan and, besides, would not be specifically Christian.

Once more it is St. Thomas who shows us the true answer: God is the last end of all things, the *Omega* of the ascent of the whole universe. And how do things achieve this ascent? As we have already seen, they do it by accomplishing the ends for which they were made, and this means that they do the will of God, that they become, in some way, like the divine will. Thus the ultimate end of every creature, man included, is to become like God in an infinite variety of degrees because of the infinite, inexhaustible riches of the divine model and of the divine perfections accomplished in creatures.

Matter obviously already bears the mark of the divine Spirit, as we saw before, but can it not manifest this more clearly? Can't it go one step more in its resemblance to God? It can, but only on condition that it receives a new infusion of the Spirit that uses the original trace and raises it to a higher coefficient. And it is man who gives matter this enriching infusion by his science and technology.

That is the basic motive that makes of human work, especially scientific work, an act with a religious value. It humanizes matter; it impregnates it with spirit (as Leo XIII said). And just as man, particularly as redeemed by Christ, is the clearest and most perfect image of God, so, too, when matter is marked with man's seal, it is raised in dignity, for the more it becomes like man, the more it resembles God.

It is in this theological context that the classical phrase used by Pius XII, "Labor carries out the work begun by God," takes on its full meaning. Human work is not creative in the sense that it produces something new, since it must always make use of material things whose characteristics it exploits. But it is creative because it produces in matter a greater resemblance to God, creating in it a new religious value. Science, particularly because of the revolution it began, the new forms it gives matter, and the mastery it has over the forces of nature, is doing truly spiritual work.

Just as Christ is the principal agent in this restoration of all things and in accomplishing God's plan, so too the scientific researcher cooperates closely by his efforts with the Lord's earthly work. Hence, he does not have to leave his laboratory to find God; God is already present in the object of his research and asks to be recognized and loved there. Not only that, but the scientist's very activity enters into participation with Christ's work in the world.

There are many other aspects of the matter to be considered, but they are concerned rather with human "work." At any rate, they are all rooted in this basic teaching. As for the scientist, the special, basic meaning of his efforts—the greater intelligibility of matter—gives his work as high a dignity as any human labor.[18] Among all workers who exercise a sort of mediation (even a "priesthood" in the broad sense) between nature and God, co-operating with Christ's action, the scientific worker is certainly the one who plays this role most effectively, because basically all other human efforts depend on him (technology uses science). He is at their very source, giving them the power to control matter because he himself has already penetrated the secrets that it conceals.

It is clear, then, that Catholicism, by its very nature, welcomes scientific progress. If in the course of history the contrary impression may have been given, it was due to some of the Church's representatives—or was rather the result of a prudence that later may have turned out to be excessive but that must be judged in the historical context (which was often complex). This was the case in the famous trial of Galileo, about which we shall speak later.[19]

2. Scientific Life and Life in the Church

We must pursue to the very end this union of the life of the scientist with that of the believer. As we have already insisted, this vital union must not stop at the threshold of Christianity, that is, at a simple reference to a vague notion of God. We must go to Christ, to find in him the justification for our endeavors—an invitation not only to adore the Creator but also to participate in the redemptive work of the God-man.

[18] That is why classical theology teaches that intellectual work cannot be paid for, since its dignity cannot be valued in terms of money. When we speak of paying for such work, we call it a salary or honorarium for the support of the person who works with his brain rather than his hands. This is somewhat the same as the idea behind the stipend for Mass. The stipend is not the price of the Mass, which has an infinite value.

[19] P. Duhem, the great historian of the sciences, has clearly pointed out the indirect role played by Christianity in the birth of Western science: "In the name of Christian teaching, the Fathers of the Church struck at the pagan philosophies on points which we today regard as more metaphysical than physical but which contained the cornerstones of ancient physics, such as the theory of eternal primary matter, or belief in the power of the stars over sublunary things, or in the pacing of the world's life to the rhythm of the Great Year. By thus attacking and exploding the cosmologies of the peripatetics, the stoics, and the neo-Platonists, the Fathers of the Church cleared the ground for modern science." (*Le Système du Monde*, Vol. I [Herman], p. 408).

But where can we find Christ? We can find him in his Church, which is not merely a group of people who profess the same faith but is Christ himself extending his work through time and space. So, when we speak of Christ's acting in the world, we must not imagine him acting from the heights of heaven on this lowly earth. His action takes place in as concrete and visible a manner as it did nearly two thousand years ago when he walked the roads of Palestine. It is exercised through the Church, which is a real organism and not merely a juridical entity; an organism animated by the same life as its founder (divine life in the Holy Spirit), whose message and supernatural efficacy it brings to the ends of the earth.[20]

[20] Like every living organism, Christ's Church must grow and develop. This is the answer to the current objection, started by Protestants, against the present-day Catholic Church: that she seems so different in structure, institutions, and juridical aspect from the primitive Church which was, on the contrary, so simple that the central power did not seem so entrenched as it is in our day. The answer to this objection is in the Gospel itself, where the kingdom of God is compared to a small seed that grows into a large tree. A seed does not contain a miniature tree; it does not have roots, trunk, or leaves on a very small scale; yet the seed and the tree that will come from it are one and the same being. The appearance of and differentiation between new organs is the law of every living thing. This objection presupposes that the Church should always remain a seed, which would be contradictory. Thus, every attempt to return to antique forms (archeologism) is illogical. The only permanent element in the Church is her soul, the Holy Spirit, who manifests his permanence by the stability of the Faith (progressive explanation of the deposit of Faith, revealed in the scriptures, by definitions in the course of history), and by the stability of the sacraments (in different liturgies) and basic institutions (the papacy, episcopal college, etc.).

Therefore it was natural that the Church, a simple seed in apostolic times, did not then have the organization of the Church of the twentieth century, which is a mighty tree. When a tree spreads its branches, its trunk must grow proportionately to bear the new burden. So too the Church, spreading to the ends of the earth, has to increase and reinforce her central power, the Holy See. Otherwise, she would betray her very nature and her message. This is all the more necessary because, in speaking to a diversity of races and cultures, she runs the risk of absorbing foreign elements and causing misunderstandings which would result in schisms. A reinforcement of the centralizing unity of the Holy See (e.g., by keeping Latin as her official language) should match the geographic spread of the Church.

On the other hand, the Church has another aspect. Because of the power given to the bishops (who are not mere delegates of the Holy See), and because of the latitude allowed to local customs and laws, the Church, like a true organism, shows great suppleness and real decentralization.

If the Christian scientist wants to participate effectively in Christ's work, he must do it through the Church. He cannot hope to attain unity in his life and help in the ascent of all things toward God unless he lives the life of the Church, taken in all its dimensions.

Even if all the conceptual and sociological obstacles are removed (and that is what we tried to do in the first part of this book), the scientist will not find the source of this life within himself. By definition this life is supernatural and hence he must, in all humility and with firm conviction, seek it in the living Church—which is Christ coming to him, by prayer, the practice of his religion, the life of the sacraments, and especially the Mass.

We cannot describe here in detail all the aspects of this life in the Church, but we can indicate two important points.

First, the scientist must never forget the risk he runs of allowing himself to be caught off guard. He knows that dealing with creatures has its dangers and requires a certain minimum of vigilance. In his domain the risk is very real because of the ease with which he can be enraptured by research on material things and the propensity to judge everything else in the light of that research. To avoid this risk, he must never forget that the life of religion can develop only in an atmosphere of recollection; hence the necessity of preserving within himself a zone of interior silence in the midst of all his work. This will allow him to keep himself in a continual state of "conversion," which is indispensable to his ideal. Since by definition his life as a Christian and a scientist must be a cooperation in the return of the universe to God, he must obviously start with himself, and he can reach his goal only by cultivating a habit of prayer and close union with God.

Next, one particular feature of his faith demands special attention, namely, the communal nature of his life in the Church. The Christian does not save himself alone but in common with his brothers in Christ, in the bosom of the Church. This means not only that he should join his personal prayer to the community practices (the liturgical life, parish life, etc.), but also that he should feel that all those who collaborate with him, from his colleagues in research to the janitor at the laboratory, are united with him in his work.

Scientific research normally leads to this atmosphere. We saw in our first chapter that at present this seems to happen only with homogeneous teams of researchers. Hence, it is a question of seeing in this need for unity an opening for the true charity of Christ, the foundation of communal life. But we must remember that the word "charity" has become so devalued by "do-gooders" (it has come to mean mere almsgiving), that we must take care to give it its original meaning of true brotherly love. All men have been called by Christ to be the adopted sons of God; consequently, a profound relationship exists between them, a relationship that goes far beyond the demands of a simple solidarity based on their common human nature. That is why, outside the climate of Christianity, the brotherhood of man has no foundation, as existentialism has so clearly shown; for Sartre, "Hell is other people." Taken in themselves, two men are as much strangers to each other as are any two animals of the same species. If they are to be called brothers, we must presuppose a higher bond between them, some kind of common fatherhood. So, unless we wish to hark back to Adam, which would be going rather far, we can logically find such a fatherhood in God alone; not in God known solely through reason (a Creator and not a Father), but in God as announced by Christ, introducing all men into the intimacy of his divine life. Two atheists who act like brothers implicitly attest to this divine fatherhood and, despite their atheism, bear witness to God.

We can understand, therefore, that this commandment of charity is at the very heart of Christianity and that, as Christ commanded, true Christians should be known by the way they practice charity. Hence, the believing scientist's testimony must always be rooted in charity, and he can have unity in his own life only by helping to restore it to the lives of others.

Accordingly, his charity should be in every way a *missionary* charity, not in the sense of proselytizing but in the sense of wanting to radiate faith and love, which of themselves demand to be radiated (if they are genuine) as witnesses to God's love for us. The normal way to give this witness in the Church is Catholic Action. A believing scientist should never refuse to participate in such action whether it be of a general or a specific nature, unless he has very special reasons. The unity of his life is not an intimate and personal affair. Just as a human being develops biologically and socially only in an appropriate atmosphere, and just as the scientist's profession consists only in working as a member of a team, so too does his religious life require this dimension. Originating in Christ, it must radiate outward, bearing witness in common with other Christians, thus becoming fully a testimony to the Church. The modern world has need of this testimony, and the scientist, like everyone else, should be careful to give it, in union with the hierarchy of the Church. This may sometimes demand courage and self-sacrifice, but it is the yardstick for measuring the depth of the unity he has achieved in his life.

3. Note on Galileo's Trial

Throughout the Middle Ages, biblical commentaries on the origin of the world adopted the old astronomical system of Ptolemy, which was very complicated in its attempt to explain the different movements of the heavenly bodies by the crystal spheres that supported them. The bible, by placing man at the summit of creation, seemed to give the earth a privileged place in the universe. Ptolemy's system, by putting the earth at the center of the universe (geocentrism), seemed to bear out this religious viewpoint, and men's minds became so accustomed to it that the geocentric system seemed to be taken for granted and to form an integral part of religious faith.

But from the sixteenth century on, religious men such as Copernicus, who was a Canon of Cracow, did not hesitate to propose another system, putting the sun at the center of the universe (heliocentrism). This system gained popularity because of the authority of Galileo, who was inspired more by a stroke of genius than by the force of proofs which later turned out to be erroneous. His condemnation by the Holy Office was by no means an infallible decree, for the Holy Office was merely a Congregation whose role was, above all, to regulate the government of the Church and to maintain the discipline of the Faith among the faithful.

Now, there was a danger that the faithful, accustomed for centuries to connect the geocentric system with religion, would find the tranquillity of their faith deeply disturbed by the new hypothesis, which, although unproved, was still being disseminated as a certainty and backed by a reputable scientist. We can compare the prudent reaction of the Holy Office to that of a mother who asks her older children to wait for information about certain things until she can speak to the younger ones, who cannot yet be safely told about such matters. There is therefore no room for speaking about expediency here; instead we should consider the Holy Office's sense of responsibility. It had to take account of the social and religious climate before accepting as truth something that was still hypothetical. On Galileo's trial see the excellent summation given by R. Lenoble in *Histoire de la Science* (Gallimard, 1957), p. 476, and Jerome J. Langford, *Galileo, Science and the Church* (Desclee Co., Inc.).

VI
AN EXAMPLE OF UNITY:
TEILHARD DE CHARDIN

Before ending this book, it may be useful to consider briefly a concrete illustration of the union between the life of the scientist and that of the believer. Where could we find a better example of this union than in the life and thought of Teilhard de Chardin? We do not propose to summarize the wide sweep of his thought in a few pages, nor is there any need for us to do so since there are many authoritative introductions to it.[1] We simply wish to show that Teilhard lived intensely the life of a priest and the life of a scientific researcher, never separating them, and that he did this by drawing upon the true sources of unity whose traditional importance we have recalled in the preceding pages.

But first, because of the amount of discussion caused by his teaching and by certain difficulties inherent in it, we must make some observations about his method of approach, for his influence on the modern world has been so great that a believing scientist cannot afford to ignore or misunderstand it.

[1] See the basic work by C. Cuenot, *Teilhard de Chardin* (Baltimore, Helicon, 1965). The list of books on Teilhard is growing at such a rate that it would be useless to try to list them all. As introductions, the best studies are still C. Tresmontant's *Pierre Teilhard de Chardin* (Baltimore, Helicon, 1959), and N. M. Wildier's *Teilhard de Chardin* (Editions Universitaires, 1960). See also the great work by H. de Lubac, *Teilhard de Chardin: The Man and His Meaning* (New York, Hawthorn Books, Inc., 1965).

I. UNDERSTANDING TEILHARD

If we are to have a balanced judgment of him and understand the meaning of his work, we must first get a true perspective on his whole life.

1. A Missionary Vocation in the Deepest Sense

When we realize the importance of his writings, both scientific and religious, we may be tempted to read them as coming from the pen of a quiet professor, working peacefully in his study, somebody one could ask to account for the conceptual exposition of his ideas. But that is the opposite of the reality, for Teilhard was actually a missionary aflame with zeal, a tireless traveler pursuing with equal intensity two objects that were really only one in his eyes—scientific research of such high quality that it made him the outstanding international expert in prehistory, and an ever-deepening encounter with God in Christ.

But how can we speak about a missionary vocation in this context? Two things explain this vocation and its special nature. First, Teilhard spent the greater part of his life among scientists of all nations. They had remarkable natural gifts but they were generally unbelievers. At the same time, his experience in China showed him that hundreds of millions of men could live outside the influence of Christianity. He could not remain untouched by both the unbelief of the Western elite who had lost the zest of living and the practical paganism of the teeming peoples of Asia.

This twofold experience gave rise to Teilhard's vocation—to give back to these men the meaning of life and to find a common center of thought and life for them. In other words, he wanted to make them discover the meaning of a divine absolute, that unique and necessary reality, whose infinite plenitude he himself experienced. The desire to communicate to others the inner fire that illuminated him, to reconcile the whole man and all his needs with the divine—that explains Teilhard's life. Everything else was only a means to serve this great vocation.

2. Science, the Natural Meeting Ground

But how was he to make his message heard? How was he to awaken men's minds and hearts to the true meaning of life? That was Teilhard's great intuition; he had to find a meeting place, a common ground to which no one, whether agnostic or unbeliever, could refuse to come, a place accessible to all. He found what he wanted in science, or rather in the great intuitions of modern science. But this word causes some anxious people to raise their arms to heaven and summons up before them the specter of concordism. They forget that, from St. Paul to St. Thomas to Pius XII, it has been a tradition as old as Christianity to find traces of God in his works. Even if these traces are not visible on the level of scientific method, they can be seen by anyone who raises himself ever so slightly above the data of science. And Teilhard, one of the masters of science, found it legitimate to use one of his great intuitions for his plan.[2] Since the religious individualism resulting from the Renaissance appeared, we have so forgotten the spirituality of a man like St. Francis of Assisi that instinctively, and in a kind of Jansenistic reflex, we are astounded by what we regard as an audacious undertaking.

Some would still have pardoned Teilhard if he had contented himself with reediting the classical proofs of the existence of God. But instead, with a profound sense of theology, he selected the one proof that he believed could most easily be integrated into a scientific context (the proof from finality), and presented it in such a natural way in this new context that many believers did not recognize it, accustomed as they were to a stereotyped presentation. This scientific context was evolution, and all the philosophico-religious confusion of the last century was against Teilhard. The true nature of divine causality, respecting and making use of created causality, had been so forgotten that the doctrine of evolution seemed irreconcilable with the Faith. Evolution had been monopolized by the materialists, and many people did not see that it could serve as ground for an encounter with God. We did not use it in

2 This is one thing that explains the opposition of certain spiritualist thinkers (of a Cartesian type), whose ignorance of Thomism and the biblical renewal is equaled only by their contempt for science and their pretensions to be the representatives of the modern Catholic intelligentsia.

this way in chapter four of this book, but waited to say something about it until a little later, because we have chosen a different point of departure, more physical than biological.

Moreover, Teilhard, while reviving a great tradition, had the audacity to want to integrate Christ and his Church into his vision. Since the time of the old deism of the eighteenth century, which penetrated the romantic religious renaissance so deeply, Christians have been in the habit of thinking that the Son of God made man had nothing to do with the universe apart from humanity, although "it is the same Word of God who created the world and who has come to lead it to its fulfillment," [3] as we have recalled in the preceding chapter.

3. Teilhard's Special Point of View

But this is not the full extent of Teilhard's originality. He began his project from a point of view so fresh that he confused many of his readers who were used to a one-sided outlook, and the majority of the critics that have attacked him start from a complete misunderstanding of this new perspective.

What is this new perspective? Since Teilhard's aim was to make himself clear mainly to unbelievers and since he wished to remain on the scientific level, he obviously could not expound the Faith in an "insider's" terms. That would have been self-contradictory. He had to try to give the most exact view of the Faith possible from outside, while necessarily leaving unclear certain aspects of it (e.g., sin), upon which the attention of Christians had sometimes been too firmly fixed. Such an attitude is perfectly logical and orthodox. From the moment that one believes that God acts in the world and knows that Christ is the great agent and mediator of the restoration of all things and of their ascent to God, it is normal that he should search nature for traces or indications of this action, not on the level of phenomena but on that of great perspectives such as evolution. Otherwise the words no longer mean anything. Confining God and Christ to the domain of the individual con-

---

[3] J. Daniélou, "Signification de Teilhard de Chardin" in *Etudes*, February, 1962, p. 152. This is one of the clearest and most authoritative studies of the content of Teilhard's thought.

science, or placing them in an inaccessible heaven, would result in driving them from the world, the great workshop, after all, of their activity *ad extra*.

Because he adopted this missionary outlook, Teilhard could no longer use the terminology of the Scholastics. This terminology is, of course, very useful for a rigorous exposition of Christian teaching "from inside," and we have tried to use it thus in the preceding pages. But if Teilhard had employed it, unbelievers would not have understood him. So he has been accused of using philosophy without knowing that he was doing so, as if this could be a reproach. To demand that philosophy must always call itself philosophy and use a specialized vocabulary would be to reduce its role drastically. Of course philosophy, like theology, must have its own language for its systematic explanations. But in his universal role, a philosopher, in order to make himself understood, can legitimately adopt a different literary style by means of which he can pass on his message; and if he does so unconsciously, that only proves his mastery of the situation. Many thinkers, from Plato to Gabriel Marcel and Sartre, have used dialogue or the theatre to awaken their audiences to the vital importance of their message.[4]

Thus it seems to us that in Teilhard's case we should, to some degree, apply the doctrine of literary types which has been used so successfully in scripture study and which is the basis of literary criticism. Many people have spoken against Teilhard as if he had been acting as a professional theologian, and they have reproached him for leaving out this or that particular point. But we must not take his work for something he never intended it to be—a systematic teaching of the Faith. He himself warned his readers about this: "No one should seek to find in these pages an explanation of the world but only an introduction to such an explanation. . . .

4 Several times Teilhard declared that he did not wish to play the philosopher in his works, and we can easily understand why when we remember the discredit into which contemporary philosophy had fallen among the scientists to whom Teilhard was speaking. He especially did not want to give the impression that he was appealing to that philosophy which, in his opinion, still belonged to an era before Galileo (see above, chapter four, footnote 5). But, for all that, because of his background, there was an implicit philosophy underlying his thought—a philosophy which is basically the spontaneous use of common sense and whose systematized expression is Thomism.

Beyond this first scientific explanation, the field is wide open for the reflections of the philosopher and the theologian." No one could be clearer or more straightforward than that.

Yet we may ask if it is right to say this, if it does not distort the Faith by giving only a partial explanation of it. This would certainly be the case if the explanation claimed to be complete. But if the explanation is meant to be only an introduction for outsiders, the accusation has no foundation. Thus Teilhard's work is a sort of preparation for a genuine encounter with Christianity; and "preparation" is a good word because Teilhard was very much aware of his role, which was to facilitate the reconciliation of modern man, who is steeped in and fashioned by science, with the whole Christian faith. Teilhard did this by showing in a sweeping vision the possible convergence of the scientific synthesis with the Christian synthesis. This is not to say that they are on the same plane, but rather that science has within it an indication, a call, that should render the Faith more appealing. And when we realize and measure the depth of the gulf between the Church and the modern world, we will see that it would be unpardonable to sabotage a serious effort to reconcile them by making petty criticisms.[5]

II. TEILHARD'S TEACHING

We shall here summarize a few elements of Teilhard's thoughts that are particularly striking.

1. The Sense of the Absolute

In the preceding pages we have had occasion to insist upon the importance of this theme for an encounter with God—this idea of

[5] Some fearful souls are frightened when they see Teilhard being adopted by the Marxists. They have exactly the same reactions as had the "do-gooders" of the last century. These people were scared to see the collectivists show an interest in the workers in the name of social justice, and they used that as an excuse for having nothing to do with the matter or for belittling Catholic social workers, whose efforts and work were often exploited by others. Such an attitude of withdrawal on the part of many Catholics only widens the breach between the Church and the modern world. We should not abandon any of Teilhard's insights and thoughts just because Marxists borrow them; on the contrary, we should use them ourselves.

the divine absolute that is basic to a real religious attitude and that obliges man to take his real place, is the foundation of the whole Christian vision of the world. Teilhard became the apostle and herald of this central doctrine, upon which everything else depends, the meaning of man as well as that of the universe. We should be grateful to him for having contributed so much to a re-evaluation of this idea and for having awakened a world oblivious of its true condition. Teilhard was well aware that the great temptation, fostered by scientific progress, was to make science an absolute and to forget that God alone has the right to this title. So it was that he tried to use science itself as a starting point for rediscovering this fundamental truth. Here is how he did it. "From my childhood the need to possess something absolute was the very axis of my interior life; . . . this preoccupation may perhaps seem unusual, but I repeat that it was ever-present. Consequently, I had the irresistible need—at once enlivening and calming—of resting in some tangible, definite thing, and I searched everywhere for this bliss-bestowing object. . . . The story of my interior life is the story of that search for realities ever more universal and perfect." At the end of his life, he repeated the same testimony, expressing in everyday language the teaching of St. Thomas about the possibility of reaching the divine absolute by starting from created, imperfect things that participate in it. He again spoke about the "irresistible need for some unique thing, sufficient and necessary; the need to be completely at ease, completely happy, to know that that one essential thing exists, of which everything else is only an accessory or rather an ornament; to know it and to rejoice unceasingly in the knowledge of its existence. Truly, if, in the course of time, I succeeded in knowing myself and in following my inclination, it was only as the result of following this note, or tint, or special taste, impossible to confuse (no matter how little one might have experienced it) with any other of the soul's desires: neither the joy of knowing, nor the joy of discovering, nor the joy of creating, nor the joy of loving—not that it differs so much from them but rather because it is of a higher order than all these emotions and because it contains them all." The essential question which Teilhard wanted each man to ask himself was: "Is life absurd or is it divine?"

2. Christ, the Omega Point

What approach does Teilhard use to make us attain this divine absolute? In the scientific part of his synthesis he takes the path most traditional in the Church, the one that St. Thomas took from Aristotle, *conceiving the absolute as the point of convergence,* the center of attraction (the final cause, as the Scholastics would say) for all the ascending movement of the universe.

And this Omega point is not taken for granted. It allows itself to be discovered by the convergence of evolution. Just as a flight of arrows aimed at a target presupposes a point toward which they are converging, so too the sense of cosmic, biological and human evolution indicates a mysterious point of convergence. Moreover, the progression that characterizes this evolutionary ascent (the law of complexity-consciousness, then reflection and spiritual thought) obliges us to see in this center of attraction *a personal, incorruptible Being, acting everywhere;* otherwise evolution would end in a void. These qualities are, in fact, those by which tradition designates God.

In the approach that we have followed in this book we have tried to meet this same God in the framework of the same classical plan, but using the descending movement as a starting point, viewing God as the ever-present source of the existence, activities, and intelligibility of beings. Now, Teilhard chose to encounter God in the *ascending* movement of these same beings. The result, however, is the same when one knows that God is the Alpha and the Omega of the whole universe. The advantage of Teilhard's position is that it can perhaps be more easily accepted by the modern mind so keenly aware of the importance of the time factor and of the irreversible character of cosmic and human history. The two movements, descending and ascending, of the universal dialectic that rules the relationship of the universe with God are therefore complementary (that is the whole basis of St. Thomas' *Summa Theologica*) and are dependent upon each other.

In the same traditional sense, Teilhard presented this divine Omega point under the aspect of Christ, the only mediator between God and the cosmic and human universe. Since Christ is the great revelation, "God with us" (Emmanuel), we should not stop at a divine representation in a vague abstract form. From the time of the incarnation onward, meeting with God takes place through Christ. Moreover, Christ exercises his unifying activity through the Church, which, by this fact, is integrated as a dominant part of this great vision.

Here, too, a person who is accustomed to reading scripture and the Fathers, and for whom theology is not a simple repetition of abstract formulas, should find in Teilhard a great teaching too often forgotten, and should be able to see this behind the unusual form he uses and his bold use of words. In order to make himself clear to men of the world, Teilhard had recourse to scientific terms and even poetic expressions that should not be pressed too far.

To some people, Teilhard's gravest error was his neglect of Christ's redemptive role and hence also of the existence of original sin or of any sin, for that matter. But the external viewpoint which Teilhard assumed would hardly allow him to emphasize the reality of sin. Perhaps he really did slight this aspect; but, as an eminent theologian has judiciously remarked, we must not exaggerate the matter because "if precise theological terms are lacking, the reality of sin and grace are clearly pointed out." [6]

Besides, in an age like ours when men are so easily led to despair, to see the world as absurd, such a lesson in Christian optimism is beneficial. And is it not characteristic of the prophets of any era to stress one point and leave another point in the shade? The variety of the doctrines and spiritualities in the history of the Church is founded upon presentations of the same dogmatic truths in different lights. How true this is of the attempt to present these truths to the modern unbelieving world!

3. The Primacy of Man

Since man is at the very center of the problem, we can say that all Teilhard's thought is a humanism. But what kind of humanism is it? Does it safeguard true human values, the foundation of our civilization?

Superficially considered, Teilhard's teaching could give the impression that he ran the risk of lowering the dignity of man by making him the end-product of an animal ancestry. Yet, paradoxi-

[6] J. Daniélou, *op. cit.,* p. 155.

cal as it may seem, Teilhard is among those who have tried hardest to restore to man his exceptional place in the cosmos that he had lost since Galileo and Darwin. He insisted strongly that man's coming represented a break—the appearance of reflection and the consciousness of self. (Let us recall that these are the characteristics by which traditional philosophy designated the spirituality of the soul.)

One could reproach Teilhard for not mentioning the creation of the human soul, demanded by its spiritual nature, but taking the scientific, *phenomenal* point of view as he did, he could not proclaim a truth that is inaccessible to science. Nevertheless, he did announce that truth in an equivalent way by clearly pointing out how thought and its characteristics were not a product of the animal world before the appearance of man.

This accusation would be somewhat like reproaching an embryologist because he did not speak about the creation of the human soul by God at the moment of the conception of a child. That is not his domain. On the other hand, when the fetus has become an adult, the same embryologist can diagnose the existence of a spiritual principle proving by its activity that it cannot be reduced to matter.

Man's primacy is shown especially by the ascendancy he exercises over the universe, which he subdues and directs, for he is the spearhead of evolution. This is a modern translation of the traditional biblical data. Hence Teilhard is led to insist on the importance and gravity of the earthly tasks that devolve upon man. In an age like ours when situation and existentialist ethics look very tempting, a similar message is useful for reviving the desire for a morality that is more objective and more biological, in the sense of the vital success of the divine plan. Here too despite appearances, Teilhard shows that he is more traditional and Thomistic than some of his critics.

III. CONCLUSION

In the new world being built, in which science and technology reign, too many Christians have adopted an ostrich-like attitude:

taking refuge in the darkness of negation, refusing to be present in the world, refusing even to ask themselves whether or not the Gospel still has a part to play. It was Teilhard's great function to recall man's true greatness in the pursuit of the divine absolute and, at the same time, to wish to place Christ and the Church in the very center of the world without minimizing the supernatural transcendence of their message.

Obviously, in doing this Teilhard perhaps played havoc with old methods and rigid routine, but he did it with missionary ardor, aware of the gravity of the times and of what was at stake and keeping to the essentials, which he had to restore at all costs. In short, he opened to us the path of reconciliation between the Church and the world. It is up to us to follow that path, to correct it if necessary, and to complete what has been begun.[7]

[7] The believing scientist, knowing that Teilhard's thought is above all a vision "from outside," will be careful to supplement it by a deep knowledge of his Faith, a task in which this book has tried to help him.

CONCLUSION

We have reached the end of our search. A real union between the life of a scientist and the life of faith seems not only to be possible but even to be demanded by the very nature of things.

In fact, science now more than ever needs this addition of the soul that Bergson called for. Given a larger role and invested with formidable responsibility, science cannot remain shut up in its own concerns. It must open out onto a wider horizon which alone can give it meaning and keep it in the service of mankind. This is what the great scientist Paul Langevin seems to have acknowledged when he asked: "Will the human species have the intelligence, the imagination and the will necessary to live there and change its organism, by evolution or by mutation, or will it perish, the victim of itself and its own effort, as other species have done before it?" [1]

Science alone is not sufficient to prevent man from being led to his ruin or to bring about a change in him. A factor of another order is needed and, at the same time, the real center of attraction toward which he is ascending must be better known. Only Christianity, by its universal character, by the breadth of its demands, and especially by the supernatural dynamism it contains, can give modern man effective help.

The believing scientist today has been given an exalted but formidable mission that binds him to be present actively and alertly in the middle of the world now being built, and requires him to direct all his efforts toward attaining man's real destiny. In conclusion, we can sum up the characteristics of this mission by saying that it must be both a temporal commitment and a supernatural hope.

[1] P. Langevin, Preface to *L'Evolution humaine* (Quillet).

A Temporal Commitment

The whole spirit of our approach has been the opposite of the evasion that many believers have adopted too easily, contrary to the spirit of the Gospel which requires the Christian to be the salt of the earth. But salt should not remain unused; to play its part it must penetrate deeply into the food it is supposed to flavor. So too the Christian, according to the place he occupies in the world's scheme, should be in the forefront, in the very first line of progress. In order to do that he must experience all the aspirations, anguish, pains, and joys of the pioneer. The believing scientist will derive from this call on his faith a powerful stimulant for his own research.

This commitment is of a temporal nature and is the mission proper to the laity—to insure the Church's presence in the building up of the earthly city. Hence, it is a question of understanding clearly that this commitment is required not only in relation to the laws of the world but by the very structure of Christianity. The kingdom of heaven begins here below; it is built up in men's hearts and from there, using their earthly condition, it becomes the natural, perishable substructure of a supernatural edifice that culminates in a different world, that of the heavenly city. "For, the more firmly his feet are planted upon the ground as he imposes his rule over the universe, the more humus our Christian life has, the more deeply rooted it is, so much the more plentifully the sap will flow, so much the richer the fruits will be. Any new conquest by the sons of Adam enlarges the sphere of God's redemptive work: are not all things, whether on earth or in heaven, to be reconciled to him through his blood shed on the cross (see Col. 1, 20)?" [2]

Christian Hope

The Christian engaged in this temporal activity must obviously draw the conviction and dynamism he needs from the virtues of faith and charity. But the virtue that perhaps best characterizes the ambiguity of his position is hope. What is hope? Certainly its direct object is God and his kingdom, but since God's will and the

[2] E. Beaucamp, *op. cit.,* p. 131.

demands of this kingdom have a bearing also on earthly tasks to be done, this supernatural virtue must concern itself in some way with all the natural hopes of humanity that have been aroused by progress and science.

This virtue of hope, then, far from detaching the Christian completely from his daily work and focusing his attention on heaven alone, makes it his duty to do his work to the full. Pius XII stressed this in his Christmas message in 1957: "It should even be considered a shame [for the Christian] to allow himself to be surpassed by God's enemies in devotion to work, the spirit of enterprise and even of sacrifice. There are no territories closed or directions forbidden to the Christian's action." And the pope defined this action in these words: "Therefore, the vocation of Christianity is not an invitation from God to mere aesthetic pleasure in contemplating his wonderful order, but the compelling call to unceasing action, austere and fully directed toward all aspects of life." [3]

Thus, Christian hope seems the best stimulant toward effective temporal action and, at the same time, a guarantee that this action will retain its proper place; that is to say, that it will remain at the service of a higher cause, the principal object of this virtue, namely, the kingdom of heaven.

The cosmic extension of the redemption brought by Christ makes this teaching more precise by placing the earthly role of hope in a christocentric context. Christ, the perfect man, by assuming in his divine Person all human and earthly values, has given them a new appearance by his resurrection and his victory over sin. He allows man to fulfill more purely and effectively his role as intermediary for created things, so that he may make of that role a still more striking testimony to God's greatness and goodness. Thus Christ, who is the pledge of Christian hope, is also the pledge of true human progress, which he alone can prevent from turning into misfortune for man.

Faced with this human hope, the Christian cannot have an inferiority complex, compared with the Marxist, for example. The

[3] This Christmas message of 1957 has great significance. There is a good commentary on it by Fr. Heckel, in *Cahiers d'action religieuse et sociale,* No. 248, June 15, 1958 (Spes).

Christian, more than the Marxist, has a real stake in working effectively for the progress of humanity; for he knows that, with Christ, he has the certainty of furthering this progress, this human hope, along its proper path, the one which leads toward man's true good instead of to a new enslavement. Thus warned by the demands of the Faith, he will not allow himself to be carried away by the intoxication of science because he knows that his efforts, in the very midst of his research, are turned toward a higher, imperishable end.

Because of all these characteristics, the committed Christian, particularly the scientist, finds himself in a situation that is rather ambiguous. He must undertake wholeheartedly an earthly task that is often captivating, and yet he must always be careful to retain a certain independence from it. He knows that, despite its attraction, it is temporal and passing, and that his mind and heart must tend, through it, toward an imperishable Reality. But, knowing that Christ is with him, he can be daring, recalling St. Paul's words: "For all things are yours, whether . . . life, or death; or things present, or things to come—all are yours, and you are Christ's and Christ is God's" (1 Cor. 3, 22-23).

APPENDICES

1. Is There Such a Thing as Artificial Thought?

One of the most spectacular aspects of modern science is certainly the appearance of artificial brains, electronic computers whose feats stagger the imagination, for they can do in minutes calculations that would take several mathematicians their whole lives to finish. Not only that, but their ever-increasing use in all sections of human activity (economic, military, political, and even literary and artistic) poses the problem of their relationship to the human mind. Are they not proof that thought can be begotten of matter?

Upon closer examination, we see that the operations of these electronic brains, despite their extraordinary features, are limited to the purely material and that it is wrong to speak of thought in connection with them. What are, in fact, the phases of the operations they perform? First, they must be given problems, and for that, problems must be conceived. Then the problems must be solved; and finally, the results must be interpreted. Now, computers can perform only the second of the three steps. As Einstein said, "It's all very well to talk of machines; they can solve all the problems one wants, but they will never be able to pose a problem." In fact, the computer is simply a tool. It cannot pass, by means of thought, from the concrete to the abstract. It is merely the reflection of its inventor's thought, its essential role being to store the facts fed into it and to combine them, according to a predetermined program, with extraordinary speed. Man stands at the beginning and at the end of this process, making it all possible

by the meaning he puts into it. Above all, he is present at the heart
of the machine. He conceived and made it in order to free his own
mind from the more material of its functions.

2. Miracles and the Laws of Nature

If there is one subject on which science and religion do not see
eye to eye, it is the subject of miracles. To the layman, miracles
are, above all, extraordinary occurrences, overthrowing the laws of
nature and escaping their rule. When miracles are viewed in this
way, they can only be a scandal and a humiliation for the scientist.

Actually miracles are quite different. They are, more than anything else, religious signs, calls to man to stir him from his torpor,
to awaken him to a spiritual mystery. The material starting point
of a miracle is therefore an event capable of provoking this reaction by reason of its strangeness. For a believer who is seeking to
meet God everywhere, everything can be called a miracle, that is, a
sign or trace of God. (See chapter four.)

But, in the strict sense, a miracle presupposes an abnormal
phenomenon or one that cannot be attributed to an immediate
cause; therefore it is an invitation for men to see in it God's special
intervention, either to show his presence more clearly or to authen-
ticate a spiritual message. Hence a miracle presupposes in the
person who sees it a basic good faith and especially a receptivity to
spiritual things. (Even Christ's miracles did not convert the Jewish
masses of his day but only a spiritual elite.)

Yet how are we to explain the material miraculous event? We
must not forget that because of the interpenetration of matter and
spirit, spirit can act on matter. (See chapter three.) Man is a
good example of this. Each time anyone, by an act of free will,
brings about an external physical change, the world receives this
change somewhat as an absolute start and includes it in the unfolding of the phenomena that follow from it. With greater reason the
same can be said of God, who can easily be the starting point of
a new causal series or who can use a causality unsuspected by the
observer.

Moreover, the Church has always been very conservative in

the matter of miracles. She knows that God ordinarily shows himself in the determinism of nature, the work of his hands (and obviously also in the vitality of the mystical body), and she is unwilling to see him interfering at every turn with the laws that are the expression of his will. In addition, when faced with a miraculous event, one could limit himself to saying simply that it is inexplicable in the light of our present knowledge of the laws of nature.

3. Space Flight and Other Inhabited Worlds

The success of manned space flights has made astronautics a practical science and has brought it out of the realm of pure fiction, opening to us the exciting possibility of exploring the cosmos sooner or later. But theologians have not waited for space exploration before considering the possible existence of other worlds inhabited by intelligent beings and the problem of their religious position in relation to the teachings of the Faith.

The problem is a vast one, and so we shall content ourselves with saying at the outset that the possibility of such worlds existing does not contradict the Faith. Moreover, theologians have used the full resources of their imagination to envisage all the possible conditions of these astral beings from the point of view of the Faith, salvation, grace, and especially their relationship to Christ. In particular they have asked whether the redemption is limited to the inhabitants of this globe because of their descent from Adam (original sin) or whether it has a cosmic application. Some theologians have even been happy to have the chance to imagine that on some far-off planet there may exist a humanity in the state of pure nature, which does not exist on earth.

The interesting thing about this problem is perhaps the way it shows how a technique as secular as astronautics can pose specifically religious questions. The essential point to remember is that it demonstrates very clearly man's responsibility and the greatness of his mission in helping all creatures to ascend to God through Christ. It may be that astronautics opens to this mission the vast perspective of the whole universe.